STORYTELLING
FROM THE BIBLE

Make scripture live for all ages
through the art of storytelling

MERIWETHER PUBLISHING LTD.
Colorado Springs, Colorado

Meriwether Publishing Ltd., Publisher
P.O. Box 7710
Colorado Springs, CO 80933

Editor: Arthur Zapel, Rhonda Wray
Cover design: Michelle Z. Gallardo

Library of Congress Cataloging-in-Publication Data

Litherland, Janet.
    Storytelling from the Bible : make scripture live for all ages through the art of storytelling / by Janet Litherland.
        p.   cm.
    Includes bibliographical references.
    ISBN 0-916260-80-1 : $9.95
    1. Bible stories. 2. Storytelling in Christian education.
3. Bible stories, English.   I. Title.
BS546.L583   1991
220.9'505--dc20   91-29871
                                                                                              CIP

This one's for
Laura, Celeste, Lady, John, and Bob

Preface

In selecting the stories for this book I had two objectives: that as many books as possible would be represented, and that the stories would be those less familiar to the reader-storyteller. As it turned out, the first objective was more difficult to achieve than the second. Several of the New Testament books, such as Paul's epistles, are sermons or letters and do not contain specific stories. In these cases I extracted what I found to be fascinating pieces of information and, through research, built them into stories that are as accurate as I could make them.

For example, in III John, Diotrephes is described as a church leader who behaves very badly. The scripture does not say why he behaves as he does, but close examination of the customs and activities of the time provides a plausible explanation. If you, the reader-storyteller, will allow me this liberty, you will discover a wealth of new material in this book. Instead of the story of Judas Iscariot's betrayal of Jesus, you will find the story of the replacing of Judas Iscariot. Instead of a sermon from Paul's letter to the Romans, you will find the story of Phoebe, the courageous woman who delivered Paul's letter to the Romans. And in the Old Testament, instead of the story of Esther, you will learn about her predecessor, Queen Vashti, and why she was dethroned.

At the end of each story I have provided some thoughts which may be used as discussion-starters if desired.

With regard to research, I am deeply grateful for the books and Bibles listed in the Bibliography, which provided essential background material, and especially for *Good News Bible*, from which biblical quotes are taken and adaptations made.

J.L.

Table of Contents

PART III: THE NEW TESTAMENT STORIES

PART I:
THE TELLING

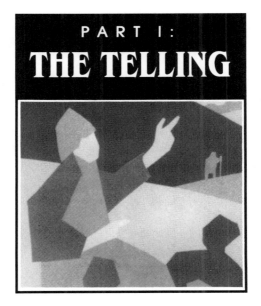

What It's All About

Sometimes preachers put us to sleep. They don't mean to, but they often settle into a pattern, of which even they seem unaware, and eventually take on a rhythmic drone that becomes more powerful than words. The rhythm lulls us, soothes us, tranquilizes us. Our minds wander down other paths, tiptoe into other places, think on other things. . .

But then, suddenly, with a different pace and a higher pitch the minister says: "The other day I was caught in a traffic jam — the strangest thing happened." We snap back, our attention riveted on . . . the story!

Stories have power. They delight, enchant, touch, teach, recall, inspire, motivate, challenge. They help us understand. They imprint a picture on our minds. Consequently, stories often pack more punch than sermons. Want to make a point or raise an issue? Tell a story. Jesus did it. He called his stories "parables."

A certain man went down from Jerusalem to Jericho and fell among thieves, which stripped him of his raiment, and wounded him, and departed, leaving him half dead. And by chance there came down a certain priest that way: and when he saw him, he passed by on the other side. And likewise a Levite, when he was at the place, came and looked on him, and passed by on the other side. But a certain Samaritan, as he journeyed, came where he was; and when he saw him, he had compassion on him, and went to him, and bound up his wounds, pouring in oil and wine, and set him on his own beast, and brought him to an inn, and took care of him. And on the morrow when he departed, he took out two pence, and gave them to the host and said unto him, "Take care of him; and whatsoever thou spendest more, when I come again, I will repay thee." Which now of these three, thinkest thou, was neighbour unto him that fell among thieves? *(KJV)*

Stories differ greatly, depending on the teller. *Good News Bible*, the American Bible Society's translation of the New Testament, presents the Good Samaritan with these words:

There was once a man who was going down from Jerusalem to Jericho when robbers attacked him, stripped him, and beat him up, leaving him half dead. It so happened that a priest was going down that road; but when he saw the man, he walked on by on the other side. In the same way a Levite also came there, went over and looked at the man, and then walked on by on the other side. But a Samaritan who was traveling that way came upon the man, and when he saw him, his heart was filled with pity. He went over to him, poured oil and wine on his wounds and bandaged them; then he put the man on his own animal and took him to an inn, where he took care of him. The next day he took out two silver coins and gave them to the innkeeper. "Take care of him," he told the inkeeper, "and when I come back this way, I will pay you whatever else you spend on him." In your opinion, which one of these three acted like a neighbor toward the man attacked by robbers? *(GNB, Luke 10:30-36)*

Someone else might tell the same story this way:

Once upon a time, a businessman was walking from one town to another. His car had broken down, you see. He didn't really mind the walk; it was a nice day and he was happy. But along came a motorcycle gang. Attracted by his important-looking briefcase, they decided to mug him. They beat him . . . they robbed him . . . and even took his new suede sport coat, varooming off without so much as a backward look.

Now it happened that a clergyman passed by in his car. He noticed the poor, helpless soul in the ditch, then looked at his watch. He was almost late for the Women's Society Chicken Supper and, after all, he was expected to ask the blessing. "Ah well," he

4

thought, "this is a busy road. Someone else will help." Shrugging, he hurried on.

A few moments later, another man happened on the scene. He looked at the guy in the ditch, noticing his expensive shoes. Could very well be a neighbor, he thought. But, it would be a shame to get all dirty trying to help someone who was probably dead anyway. So he went on by, pretending he hadn't seen.

But then along came a foreigner. He was walking, not because his car had broken down, but because he didn't own one. He was dusty and sweaty, and, like the others, he too was in a hurry. He was meeting some of his new buddies for an all-night poker game. Nevertheless, when he saw the poor guy in the ditch, his heart went out to him. He opened his Thermos and bathed the man's wounds with cold water. Then he gave him a bite of his bologna sandwich. After a few minutes, he helped him to his feet and supported him as, together, they walked to the nearest motel.

When the wounded man was made comfortable, the foreigner paid the motel bill in advance, promising that if any more were due, he would pay it on his way back home.

Which of these travelers was the true neighbor?*

Many stories, as they are passed from generation to generation, take on characteristics and attitudes of the times. Likewise, stories passed from culture to culture absorb elements of each culture. That is why you may hear the same stories — yes, even Bible stories — told with different slants or with different points of emphasis. Stories link us with our heritage, from who we were, to who we are, to who we will become.

*(Adapted from "A Parable," *The Clown Ministry Handbook* by Janet Litherland. Copyright© 1989, Meriwether Publishing, Ltd.)

II Samuel 12:1-4 is our earliest example of a parable, or story that teaches something.

> There were two men who lived in the same town; one was rich and the other poor. The rich man had many cattle and sheep, while the poor man had only one lamb, which he had bought. He took care of it, and it grew up in his home with his children. He would feed it some of his own food, let it drink from his cup, and hold it in his lap. The lamb was like a daughter to him. One day a visitor arrived at the rich man's home. The rich man didn't want to kill one of his own animals to fix a meal for him; instead, he took the poor man's lamb and prepared a meal for his guest. *(GNB)*

Nathan told this story to David. When David realized its meaning, he said, "I have sinned against the Lord."

Does a story need explanation? No.

One day, when my son was very young, he came home from school with a joke to tell. He told it. I laughed. Then he asked, anxiously, "Did you get it, Mom? Did you get it?"

Ministers, especially, seem to want to explain stories, to grind them in, to be sure their congregations understand ("Did you get it?"). Many times in doing this they impose an understanding or interpretation, robbing their listeners of the opportunity to think or reflect. Look at it this way: The storyteller serves the meal, but each listener takes something different from the plate. Jewish people believe *Torah lo bashamayim hi* (The Torah is not in Heaven). It is up to those on earth to use wisdom and understanding in interpreting the text. So, the teller interprets while telling, and the listener interprets while listening! And, just as no two people will tell a story the same way, no two people will listen the same way.

Jesus Himself leaves conclusions to the listener: "He that hath ears to hear, let him hear."

Choosing and Adapting Stories

A good story is a work of art. As it develops, it may inspire, enlighten, challenge, or even heal, but it must always, from beginning to end, entertain. This doesn't mean it always has to be funny. It means that it has to hold the audience's attention.

A good story is also a story worth telling: Do you like it? Does it stretch the imagination? Does it reach into human emotion? Does it satisfy? All of us have read at least one book (with a perfectly good storyline) that left us feeling empty and cheated at the end. That's not to say that every story must have a happy ending, only that it must have a satisfying ending. It should feel right.

Printed stories don't necessarily "tell" well. The test is to read them aloud. If a story easily accepts gesture, voice inflection, and a little on-the-side commentary, it will work. According to Donald Davis, a former Methodist minister and now a full-time storyteller, "The function of stories is to access the oral medium." If this is true, then we must be especially careful to choose stories that tell well.

Sometimes stories need to be adapted or changed in some way, possibly shortened or lengthened to fit a particular time frame. Or, they may need to be told in a slightly different manner to suit the listeners' age group. In order to keep the plot moving, which is essential for listeners, the descriptive material enjoyed by readers may need to be cut. Do take great care, however, not to change the intent of the story.

If you are working directly from the Bible, particularly the King James Version, it may be necessary (certainly interesting) either to update or to explain some of the obsolete words or phrases. For example:

Matthew 7:3-5, the "mote" in the eye (a piece of straw or a splinter)

Mark 10:25, the "needle's eye" (a small door in a city gate — a human could pass through easily; but a camel, even unloaded and kneeling, would find it nearly impossible).

John 1:5, "the darkness 'comprehended' it not" (could not overtake or wipe out the light).

I Corinthians 13:12, "see through a glass, darkly" (an imperfect reflection, as in a bad mirror).

shew (show)

Amen and Selah (so be it)

hosanna (save us)

hallelujah (praise be)

Modern, interpretive Bibles such as *The Good News Bible* and *The Living Bible*, also the "Cotton Patch Version" books by Clarence Jordan, present the scriptures in a more storylike fashion. For extra detail, recent Bible commentaries provide contemporary points of view, and Bible dictionaries are full of background information (clothing, food, weather, customs) to help you develop your stories.

If the allotted time is long, say, thirty to forty-five minutes, you might want to plan a "concert" or story program. You could build it around a central theme, or you could create a potpourri of short, entertaining stories. Poems and songs (especially story poems and songs) may also be included. Julie Portman and Paul Reisler, professional storytellers from Virginia, use hammer dulcimer, guitar, harp, and other musical instruments to enhance their stories. A prop or two, such as a drawing or an object related to one of the stories, can also create additional interest. Keep things simple.

When or where might bible stories be told?

- —Sunday school
- —Vacation Bible school
- —Summer camp
- —Sermons
- —Senior citizens' luncheons
- —Women's or men's meetings
- —Class parties
- —Day care
- —Elder care
- —Retreats
- —Fellowship suppers
- —Just about any place or time a group of people come together for worship, study, or fellowship

Are you worried that the audience may have heard your story before? (If it's a Bible story, they probably have!) Laura Nebel, a professional storyteller from Michigan, says, "If they've heard it before, it's a special feeling; and if they haven't heard it, that's a special feeling too."

Preparing the Storyteller (You!)

Most listeners don't just listen; they involve themselves in the plot. For this reason, the story will be more effective if you, the storyteller, tell the story as if you are a member of the group, rather than a performing actor. Relax and be yourself. Actors and stand-up comics generally need a stage with microphones and lights, costumes and props. Storytellers do not. If circumstances force you to be a "stand-up" teller (which, incidentally, is much more difficult than being a "sit-down" teller), become part of the group by moving into and through the audience. Captivate them!

Sit comfortably with your listeners, preferably on their level — a little chair with little people — so that you can watch their reactions. Making eye contact with the audience is extremely important, for storytelling, in any size group, should always be considered "one-on-one." Above all, the audience should be able to see you and hear you without having to squint or strain their ears.

Try to set a cozy scene, one without distractions, such as posters or pictures hanging around the room, or bells ringing periodically. If a disturbance occurs during the story — airplane noise, thunder, someone's "beeper" — either ignore it, holding the audience with eye contact and energy, or work the disturbance into the story. Use it.

Preparation is important, even though you will be telling the story in your own words. Ever listen to a preacher, teacher, or public speaker who you just knew was unprepared? Were you embarrassed? Restless? Very few people can speak "off-the-cuff" without making the audience uncomfortable. A storyteller is no different.

"In my own words?" you gasp.

9

With some exceptions. If the sound of the language as written is important to the story, memorize it; otherwise use your own words. For example, "Glory to God in the highest, and on earth peace, good will toward men." Memorize this. It sounds good. Obviously, a rhyming story is memorized.

"I thought I was going to memorize the whole story. Or maybe read it dramatically."

Sorry, that's not storytelling. Fact is, you shouldn't even use notes. Now don't be scared — this isn't as difficult as it sounds. Actually, there aren't any hard and fast rules or step-by-step formulae for preparing to tell stories. Each storyteller develops techniques that work for him or her. Here are, however, some basics that will help you get started.

1. Always remember that the most important thing is the story, not the teller. This will help you relax and forget about yourself.

2. Read the story over and over, visualizing as you read, until the story becomes part of you — until you can turn on the "auto pilot" and let the tale take over. Then you'll begin using your own words.

3. Map your route. That is, plan your beginning and ending sentences, and learn the sequence of events. (This keeps you from tooling down side roads and losing your way.)

4. Practice aloud until the telling seems effortless. Try sitting in front of a mirror. If you have the equipment, video-tape yourself, study the finished product, and learn from what you see. Or, audiotape your story as you want to tell it, then play the tape as you do household chores or while driving the car.

5. Try out your stories on the neighborhood children.

A few more tips:

1. Begin with short, simple stories, gradually working into longer, more complicated ones.

2. Summon plenty of inner energy!

3. Use "body language." Develop facial expressions and gestures. Just be sure they're a natural extension of your own

personality, so that you will feel comfortable. Caution: Too much of anything becomes annoying.

4. Sometimes a costume or a prop may be used. If you want to pretend you are a Bible character, telling either your own story or one you have "witnessed," a costume would be in order. If an object, such as a seashell, is important to your story, you might hold that object. In working with children, a hand puppet could be used as a "listener," possibly reacting but not speaking. (Ruth Stotter says in *Yarnspinner*, "Before you use a puppet, seriously consider whether doing so will enhance your telling.") As above, too much of anything etcetera, etcetera.

5. Speak slowly, distinctly, and loudly enough to be heard.

6. Use your natural voice, but do experiment with different voices for special characters. For example, if a gruff old man speaks in your story, lower your voice and make it a little raspy for his lines. (Do not attempt dialect. Not only is it extremely difficult to do, some members of your audience may be offended by it.)

7. Make use of the dramatic . . . pause.

8. Children love repetition. If you use a phrase over and over, you'll soon find them saying it with you. They also love big words. Explain them and use them.

9. Don't be afraid to take time in the telling. There's no hurry.

10. Briefly introduce your story: State the story's theme, tell why you chose it, or give a verbal sketch of one of the characters. Then credit the story: If you heard someone tell it, mention the teller's name. If it came from a book, mention the book. If it's a Bible story, tell your audience where it occurs in the Bible.

Jimmy Neil Smith, in *Homespun*, says, "How one tells the story is the mark of the storyteller." In other words, each storyteller has his or her own style of telling. Yours will develop as you practice and tell, practice and tell. So, please

11

understand that you don't have to tell stories in a certain way to be a "real" storyteller. You don't have to copy anyone.

And the Stories Go On. . .

From Genesis to Revelation, stories abound in the Bible. These stories were told before they were written down, and they still "tell" well today. I learned Bible stories as a very young child, not from reading them (because I hadn't yet learned to read), but because my mother and my Sunday school teachers told them to me. In turn, I told them to my children and, I expect, the same stories will continue to be heard by future generations of my family. This is called Oral Tradition. It is important.

Most of us have heard the stories of Moses in the Bulrushes, of Daniel in the Lion's Den, of Noah's Ark, of Baby Jesus in the Manger, of Feeding the Five Thousand with Loaves and Fishes, of the Resurrection of Jesus, and countless other Bible stories. In Parts II and III of this book, however, we will be exploring the less familiar, though certainly no less important, stories. We're going to s-t-r-e-t-c-h our minds and our imaginations and add exciting new vistas to our Oral Tradition!

Take my hand. I'll guide you through the streets where the disciples walk, into the neighborhood where the handsome and charming Epaphroditus lives, and into a church where strange people do some very strange things. We'll join a spy on the roof of her house, we'll meet the Queen of Sheba, have a chat with Job and a chat with Jude, and attend a real Bible times festival! Are you ready? . . .

Wait! You can't go like that! This is a trip back in time. Way back, to the first century. If you show up in jeans and Reebok shoes, you'll scare everybody half to death — they'll think the end of the world has surely come! You must blend, like I do.

Put on a tunic. It's basic. You'll also need a mantle or shawl and, oh yes, a kaffiyeh — you know, a headdress. And change into sandals, for heaven's sake!

. . .Now are you ready? Then let's go.

Try not to talk funny.

PART II:
THE OLD TESTAMENT STORIES

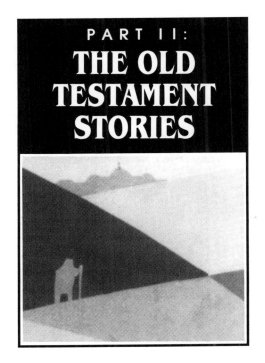

JACOB WRESTLES WITH GOD
(Genesis 32:22-32)

Jacob, as a young man, was a selfish person. He was also quiet, methodical, and very clever. He was jealous of his own brother, and by lying — even about God — he managed to steal his brother's birthright. What in the world is a *birthright?*

In Old Testament days a father gave a blessing to his first-born son. This was the custom. It included a double portion of the inheritance and the privilege of priesthood. (There were also small advantages, such as being seated first at a meal!) And, it was through the first-born son that the family name continued. Birthrights were important.

All along, Jacob's attitude had been that he should have the best of everything. If he didn't already have it, he would take it. And so he took his brother Esau's inheritance and left home. To the people in his new surroundings, he was aggressive, successful, and rich. But Jacob, in his heart, knew what he really was. He could never shake the tremendous guilt he felt because of what he had done.

After several years had passed, Jacob, the successful man, decided that it was time to return to his birthplace, time to make amends. He was a little afraid, because he knew he would meet people who would remember him as a liar and a cheat. He was also reluctant to face his brother. Would Esau forgive him?

As he approached the Jabbok River near his old home, old memories came flooding over him, old fears surfaced, and suddenly he thought that it might be wise to send everything he owned across to Esau first — sort of "test the atmosphere" before he, himself, went across. So he sent his two wives, his two mistresses, eleven children, four hundred servants, and several hundred animals, which were gifts for Esau, across the river.

It was now dark, and Jacob was alone. He had plenty of

15

time to remember, to regret, and to worry. Or did he? Suddenly, out of that vast darkness and loneliness, a man appeared. Very quickly he grabbed Jacob and tried to wrestle him to the ground. Jacob didn't recognize the man and didn't understand what it was all about. Still, he struggled with all his might. After all, he'd always been a winner.

First one went down, then the other, then one, then the other. The wrestling went on until nearly daybreak! When the strange man realized that Jacob was winning, he tried something different. He hit Jacob on the hip, throwing the hip out of joint. Still, Jacob held on.

"Let me go," said the man. "Daylight is coming."

But Jacob would not let go, because by then he had figured out who the man was. "Give me your blessing," Jacob pleaded, holding tight.

"What is your name?" the man asked.

"Jacob," he answered.

The man said, "Your name will no longer be Jacob. You have struggled with God and with men, and you have won; so your name will be Israel." Jacob had been wrestling with God!

This was not just a spiritual wrestling match. It was so intense that Jacob felt it physically. In fact, as the sun rose, he limped away — his hip was actually out of joint where God had hit him.

Jacob had also been wrestling with himself. Worst of all, he had to introduce himself to God, admitting who and what he was. That was a difficult thing to do. It took all night! But it was the only way that he could be free to go and meet his brother. What would Esau say? What would he do?

Finally, Jacob summoned the courage to cross the river. As he reached the opposite shore and limped toward home, he saw his brother Esau coming toward him — running, with his arms outstretched! Jacob was forgiven; and he wept.

This story of Jacob wrestling with God and with himself was crafted into a magnificent 14-verse poem by Charles

Wesley, first published in the year 1742. Its title is "Come, O Thou Traveler Unknown," and it has been called Wesley's finest poem. Today, it still appears in many hymnals, set to a haunting Scottish melody. Among the verses are these:

(NOTE: The verses may be spoken or sung)

> Come, O thou Traveler unknown,
> whom still I hold, but cannot see!
> My company before is gone,
> and I am left alone with thee;
> with thee all night I mean to stay
> and wrestle till the break of day.

> My prayer hath power with God; the grace
> unspeakable I now receive;
> through faith I see thee face to face,
> I see thee face to face, and live!
> In vain I have not wept and strove —
> thy nature, and thy name is Love.

What is this story *really* about?

Selfishness:

Most often we think of selfishness as being a childish trait, but there are some selfish adults in this world, too. How does selfishness hurt other people? How do you cope with a selfish person?

Cheating:

Jacob cheated his brother out of his inheritance. Some people cheat on exams or on income taxes or on other things. What would you do if you knew someone was cheating? What if their cheating improved their status but at the same time made you look bad?

Guilt:

Sometimes we do things that we're sorry for, and saying we're sorry won't fix them. We carry the guilt of those misdeeds for a long time. Is it possible to get over feeling guilty? How? If not, what can help us live with it?

Forgiveness:

Jacob was forgiven by Esau. He was also forgiven by God, after he had admitted who and what he was. That forgiveness freed him to meet not only his brother but the rest of humankind as well.

We have Christ, now, to forgive our sins. How do we get Christ's forgiveness?

Let's *talk* about it!

LET MY PEOPLE GO — I MEAN IT!
or
Ten Ways to Get Someone to Do Something
(Exodus 7-12:36)

(It is fun to have cards with "yea," "boo," etc. to cue your listeners. They will like helping you tell this story.)

This story is a melodrama with plenty of action. The stage is the land of Egypt, and the scenes are played over the course of one year in the fifteenth century, B. C. As in any good play, the characters are bigger than life. They are exciting!

There is a heroine — the Israelites, *(Yea!)* who need desperately to be rescued from slavery;

a hero — Moses, *(Yea!)* whom God empowers to carry out the rescue;

and a villain — Pharaoh, *(Boo!)* who wants to keep the Israelites in bondage. (Tied to the tracks, so to speak.)

Aaron is there to help his brother, Moses;

and a group of magicians are there to help Pharaoh.

Let's see who wins.

Our hero, Moses, *(Yea!)* was eighty years old at the time of this daring rescue. Considering that Moses *(Yea!)* lived to age one hundred and twenty, our hero was a young man. Likewise, his brother Aaron was a youthful eighty-three. With God's help, they had absolutely no trouble performing the extraordinary miracles that were needed, if they were to overpower Pharaoh. *(Boo!)*

The first thing they did, of course, was ask nicely. Moses *(Yea!)* said to Pharaoh, *(Boo!)* "The God of Israel would like you to let his people go, so that they may worship him in a new land."

Pharaoh *(Boo!)* was indignant that they should even suggest such a thing! "Let them go? My slaves?"

Of course he wouldn't let his slaves go. He was into highly ambitious building projects, and slave labor was critical to his success. . . . But he was curious.

"Why should I let them go?" he asked. "I don't know your God. I have no proof of his power."

God had anticipated this attitude and had instructed Aaron to perform a little trick. Aaron threw his cane onto the floor in front of Pharaoh, and the cane turned into a snake! *(Ooh!)*

Pharaoh *(Boo!)* just laughed and snapped his fingers for his magicians. They, too, threw down canes that turned to snakes. And, even though Aaron's snake ate the magicians' snakes, Pharaoh *(Boo!)* was stubborn. He said, "No!" He would not let the Israelites go. *(Hiss!)*

So Moses, our hero, *(Yea!)* under God's direction, began performing miracles to prove God's power. (He also wanted to scare Pharaoh *(Boo!)* into releasing the slaves.) The magicians hung around, too, because they were sure that they could duplicate any tricks this intruder might have up his sleeve.

First, Moses *(Yea!)* told Aaron to strike the water of the Nile River with his cane as Pharaoh *(Boo!)* and his magicians watched. "The water will be turned to blood," God explained. "The fish will die, and the river will stink so much that the Egyptians will not be able to drink from it." Aaron used his cane, and that is exactly what happened. *(Ooh!)*

"That's easy," said the magicians. "We, too, can turn water red and make it smell bad." And they did. *(Hiss!)*

Second, Moses *(Yea!)* said to Pharaoh, *(Boo!)* "The Lord says, 'Let my people go, so that they can worship me. If you refuse, I will punish your country by covering it with frogs. The Nile will be so full of frogs that they will leave it and go into your palace, your bedroom, your bed, the houses of your officials and your people, and even into your ovens and baking pans. They will jump on you.'" Pharaoh *(Boo!)* still refused, so

Aaron held out his cane. Frogs came up out of the water and jumped all over everything! *(Ooh!)*

"Double easy," said the magicians. And they, too, made frogs come onto the land. *(Hiss!)*

"Enough frogs!" shouted Pharaoh. *(Boo!)* "Ask your God to take away these frogs and I will let your people go." (But he was lying.)

Moses *(Yea!)* prayed, God killed the frogs, and the Egyptians swept them up into huge piles. When Pharaoh *(Boo!)* saw the frogs were dead . . . he went back on his word.

Third, Moses *(Yea!)* had Aaron hit the ground with his cane, so that all the dust in Egypt turned into gnats — stinging, biting little pests that bothered everyone.

This time the magicians failed to duplicate what they thought was a trick. They probably didn't want to anyway, since being covered in gnats is not a pleasant thing. "God has done this!" they said to the king. But Pharaoh *(Boo!)* remained stubborn.

Fourth, Moses *(Yea!)* warned Pharaoh *(Boo!)* that God would send swarms of flies to feed on the dead frogs, and that flies would be everywhere except around the Israelites. *(Yea!)* That way Pharaoh *(Boo!)* would know that the Israelites *(Yea!)* were God's people. When Pharaoh *(Boo!)* refused, the flies came. The Israelites, free of flies, cheered; and the Egyptians, swatting furiously, booed.

Moses *(Yea!)* prayed, God took away the flies . . . and again Pharaoh *(Boo!)* went back on his word. What would it take to convince this man?

Miracle Number Five: God sent a disease that killed all of the Egyptians' animals. Even this didn't convince Pharaoh. *(Boo!)* His magicians, watching in awe, were convinced. They'd given up after Miracle Number Three!

Now Moses *(Yea!)* was up to Number Six. "Take a few handfuls of ashes from a furnace," God said to Moses, *(Yea!)* "and throw them into the air in front of the king. They will spread out like fine dust over all the land of Egypt." These dust particles were to settle on the Egyptian people, producing "boils" or open sores. So Moses tossed the ashes, and the ugly boils appeared. This time the magicians stayed indoors. They couldn't stand up, because they had boils on their feet! Still, Pharaoh *(Boo!)* refused to let God's people go.

For the seventh miracle God chose an unusually violent hailstorm. Many people and animals were killed, trees were broken, and plants were bent to the ground. Only around the Israelites *(Yea!)* was there no hail.

"Pray to your God!" the king said once again. "Stop this hail, and I will let your people go." (Such a liar!)

Moses *(Yea!)* prayed, the hail stopped . . . and Pharaoh *(Boo!)* went back on his word.

The eighth miracle was really awful. *(Ooh!)* God sent a huge swarm of locusts to settle over the whole country. They covered the ground until it was black with them, and they ate everything that the hail had left, including all the fruit. Not a green thing remained.

This time Pharaoh's *(Boo!)* officials pleaded with him. "How long is this man going to give us trouble? Don't you realize that Egypt is ruined? Let these people go."

Again, Pharaoh *(Boo!)* said, "No!"

Miracle Number Nine: (Could anything be worse than a swarm of bugs? How about continual darkness?) For three days the people could not see, so they stayed in their houses, too frightened to come out. Eventually, Pharaoh *(Boo!)* said to Moses, *(Yea!)* "You and your people may go, but your sheep, goats, and cattle must stay."

Moses *(Yea!)* could be stubborn, too. He said, "No, we will not go without our animals."

This made Pharaoh *(Boo!)* very angry, because he thought he was doing Moses *(Yea!)* a big favor. "Get out of my sight!" he shouted. "Don't let me ever see you again!"

Well, he did see Moses *(Yea!)* again, just one more time — the time of the tenth miracle. This miracle was the Passover.

Israelite families were instructed to kill a lamb or young goat for a meal. They were to take blood from the animal and put it on the doorposts of their houses.

"I will go through the land of Egypt," God said to the Israelites, *(Yea!)* "killing every first-born male. . . . the blood on the doorposts will be a sign to mark the houses in which you live. When I see the blood, I will pass over you and will not harm you when I punish the Egyptians. You must celebrate this day as a religious festival to remind you of what I, the Lord, have done. Celebrate it for all time to come."

The Israelites *(Yea!)* did as they were commanded . . . and that night there was loud crying in all of Egypt. The first-borns were dead.

Finally, Pharaoh *(Boo!)* sent for Moses *(Yea!)* and Aaron. He said, "Get out, you and your Israelites! *(Yea!)* Leave my country; go and worship the Lord, as you asked. Take your sheep, goats, and cattle, and leave!"

The villain *(Boo!)* *(Hiss!)* was defeated. The hero *(Yea!)* was victorious. And the heroine *(Yea!)* was free.

"Oh, one more thing," Pharaoh said, as they were leaving. "Pray for a blessing on me."

What is this story *really* about?

Power Struggle:

Pharaoh locked himself into a power struggle with God — imagine that! Most people are interested in power. Why? What are some ways that power can be put to good use? How did Pharaoh manage to control the struggle so long — what was his technique?

Each plague was removed. How?

Stubbornness:

Everyone involved in a power struggle is stubborn. They have to be, if they want to win. But some people are stubborn all the time, over things that don't really matter that much. What makes them that way? How should we react to stubborn people?

Lying:

Pharaoh was a liar. He told several "whoppers." But that's not the same as telling "little white lies" — or is it? What do you think? Read Revelation 21:8 to see how God feels about liars.

Let's *talk* about it!

THE SCAPEGOAT
(Leviticus 16:20-22;26)

Every day we have problems. Sometimes they're huge, and sometimes they're no bigger than not having clean socks to wear. Many times we solve our problems, but often we simply get rid of them by blaming them on someone or something else. We use a scapegoat.

The origin of the term "scapegoat" is very interesting. It means, literally, a goat who "escapes" with the misdeeds, or sins, of people. The goat takes the evil deeds away, and the people are no longer bothered with them.

God ordered Aaron to prepare the first scapegoat for the Day of Atonement. He told Aaron to choose a goat, to put both of his hands on the goat's head, and to pray over it. His prayer was to be a confession of all the evils, sins, and rebellions of the people of Israel. (It must have been a long prayer!) These sins would then be transferred to the goat's head.

Next, Aaron was to appoint a man to chase the goat away to Azazel, which some Bible scholars say was a rugged cliff. The goat would fall over the cliff and die, thus ridding the people of all their sins. The man who had chased the goat was then instructed to wash his clothes, and take a bath before returning to the village. What a convenient way to get rid of the stain of sin!

Other cultures and times used different scapegoats. The Babylonians used a ram. The ancient Greeks used human scapegoats — each year they chose a man and a woman who were either deformed or criminal and ran them out of the city with whips. The Japanese, even today, transfer their misfortunes to rags and rice stalks and throw them into the river.

We, too, use scapegoats to take the blame for our shortcomings. If we lose a contest, it's because the judge (our scapegoat) was unfair. If we're late for an appointment, it's because the car (our scapegoat) wouldn't start. If we don't show up at a church meeting, it's because a family member (our scapegoat) was sick. And, if we don't have any clean socks to wear, it's because our mother, or our spouse, or our roommate forgot to wash them. It's never our fault. Today's scapegoat is often a convenient alibi.

But let's get back to the original scapegoat, the one Aaron prayed over and had someone chase to the cliff. This scapegoat formed the basis for a ritual that became, in Bible days, an annual event. Sometimes, instead of one man chasing the goat, all the people chased it. Other times, sentinels were posted along the way to signal back, reporting whether the goat reached its destination.

This was not a game. The people of Bible times were serious. They honestly believed that their sins had been transferred to the goat. It is difficult for us to understand it today, and, in fact, we cannot understand it without taking into account the prayers that accompanied the ritual. They were prayers of atonement, first ordered by God Himself.

The understanding becomes vividly clear when we consider our Lord Jesus Christ. He, too, was burdened with sin and shame. He, too, was rejected. He was driven away. And he was put to death. Over and over, as we celebrate the sacrament of Holy Communion . . . "Take, eat, this is my body," . . . and offer our prayers of atonement, the Lord Jesus Christ takes upon himself all of our sins.

Is not Christ the ultimate scapegoat?

What is this story *really* about?

Blame:

Blaming someone or something else for our own problems seems like an easy way out. How do you feel about using scapegoats? How do you think the scapegoat (if it's human) feels?

Rejection:

Scapegoats are figures of rejection. Christ, our scapegoat, was rejected. Have you ever been rejected for a job or an honor, or by someone you love? How did rejection feel to you? What are some ways to cope with rejection?

Atonement:

Atonement means to make amends for, or to satisfy a debt in some way. In Old Testament times, people paid an amount of money at the temple to make atonement for their sins. When Christ entered the picture, he radically changed the way people dealt with sin. His Crucifixion "atoned" for our failures. Atonement gives us hope.

Let's *talk* about it!

Foretelling the future was a popular activity in ancient times, and those who practiced it were called "diviners." They interpreted dreams, drew lots, studied astrology, used divining rods, and consulted the dead. Some diviners got their information by examining, or "reading," the liver of animals. None of this sounds scientific by today's standards, but many people in Bible times took it quite seriously.

Zechariah, the prophet, warned against such foolishness when he said, "People consult idols and fortunetellers, but the answers they get are lies and nonsense. The comfort they give is useless."

Moses gave an even stronger warning against the forbidden magic. "People follow the advice of those who practice divination and look for omens," he said, "but the Lord your God does not allow you to do this."

Balaam, a man from the Euphrates Valley, was a diviner. His specialty was reading livers. But Balaam was a different sort of diviner because, unlike others, he also listened to God. He didn't always obey God, but he did listen. And when it came to doing his job, he tended to mix his "divining" with the Divine. You might say he covered all his bases.

One day Baal, a Moabite king, sent messengers to Balaam for advice. He was worried about an army of Israelites who planned to attack his people.

"This horde will soon destroy everything around us, like a bull eating grass in a pasture," the king said. "They outnumber us, so please come and put a curse on them for me. Then perhaps we will be able to defeat them and drive them out of the land. I know that when you pronounce a blessing, people are blessed, and when you pronounce a curse, they are cursed."

That made Balaam feel pretty important. He decided to have the messengers stay overnight and wait for his answer.

In the meantime, God came to Balaam and asked, "Who are these men that are staying with you?"

When Balaam explained, God said, "Do not go with these men, and do not put a curse on the people of Israel, because they have my blessing."

The message was delivered to the Moabite king who was, to put it mildly, upset. He decided to try again. This time he sent an important delegation to Balaam and offered a generous payment if Balaam would return with them and pronounce the curse.

Balaam said that all of the king's silver and gold would not persuade him to disobey God; but, he would ask God one more time. (That's a trick children use with parents!)

God lost patience. "Go if you must!" he said, "But say only what I tell you to say."

So Balaam climbed on his donkey and left to visit the king. On the road, however, God did something very interesting. He put his angel in the road to block the way, but only the donkey could see the angel. This frightened the donkey and he balked. Balaam, not understanding, slapped the donkey until he started forward once more. Again the angel stood in the way. This time the donkey moved sideways, scraping Balaam's foot against a stone wall. Balaam yelled and gave the donkey a whipping. When the donkey saw the angel a third time, it gave up and lay down in the road. Then Balaam really lost his temper and began hitting the donkey with a stick.

Suddenly, the Lord gave the donkey the power of speech, and the donkey said to Balaam, "What have I done to you? Why have you beaten me these three times?"

Balaam answered, "Because you have made a fool of me! If I had a sword, I would kill you!"

The donkey replied, "Am I not the same donkey on which you have ridden all your life? Have I ever treated you like this before?"

"No," he answered.

Then the Lord let Balaam see the angel standing there, and Balaam threw himself face downward on the ground. "I have sinned," he said. "I did not know that you were standing in the road to oppose me; but now if you think it is wrong for me to go on, I will return home."

This little incident is particularly interesting because it is the only time in Old Testament literature that an animal talks, with the exception of the serpent in the Garden of Eden.

Remarkably, after going to all of this trouble with the donkey, God allowed Balaam to continue his journey, reminding him to say only what he was told.

When Balaam finally reached the palace, he instructed the king to take him to Bamoth Baal, a high place from where they could see the Israelites. There they built seven altars and sacrificed seven rams and seven bulls. (Balaam, the diviner, no doubt saved the livers for reading!)

Anxiously King Baal awaited the curse, but when the words finally came from Balaam's lips, they were a blessing!

Balaam explained, "I can only say what the Lord tells me to say."

This angered the king. "Come with me to another place," he said, "and try again."

They went to the top of Mount Pisgah, where the same thing happened, and finally to the top of Mount Peor, overlooking the desert. King Baal was sure that from this magnificent vantage point God would let Balaam pronounce his curse.

These words came out: "The nation is like a mighty lion. Whoever blesses Israel will be blessed, and whoever curses Israel will be cursed."

The king was furious! He clenched his fists and stomped his feet. "Get out of here! Go home!" he yelled. "I said I would reward you, but the Lord has kept you from getting your reward!"

"I told you," said Balaam, "that even if you gave me all the silver and gold in your palace, I would say only what the Lord told me to say."

As Balaam got ready to leave, the Lord told him to say one more thing:

"I look into the future,
And I see the nation of Israel.
A king, like a bright star,
   will arise in that nation.
Like a comet he will come from Israel."

(Pause)

"There shall come a Star out of Jacob, and a Sceptre shall rise out of Israel." . . . One of the Old Testament's most important prophecies.

Balaam didn't get that from reading livers!

What is this story *really* about?

Obedience:

Throughout the Bible, we are taught to obey — the prophets, our parents, our master, God. Balaam "sort of" obeyed God. How is his style of obedience a lot like ours, even though we're reluctant to admit it? Why do you suppose Balaam pressured God into letting him start out on the donkey? What was so important? Is it ever right not to obey?

Fortunetelling:

Have you ever been to a fortuneteller? What was it like? How did you feel about it afterward? A lot of people are serious about "horoscopes." Do you follow yours in the newspaper? If so, does it predict the way you will do something . . . or do you do something the way it predicts?

Let's *talk* about it!

Rahab was a prostitute. She was also a spy who played a prominent role in Joshua's capture of Jericho. According to rabbinic tradition, Rahab was one of the most beautiful women in the world. Like other women of her profession, she bathed herself in perfume, dressed in beautifully embroidered clothes, decorated her wrists and ankles with jingly bracelets, and was very good at "smooth talk."

Prostitutes, or "harlots," appeared throughout biblical history. Sometimes they were looked upon with disdain, shunned by townspeople, scorned, or even punished for practicing their craft. At other times and in other places, as with Rahab of Jericho, they were accepted as part of the community, and no one objected to their "business." There was only one restriction — earnings could not be used to pay tithes in the temple!

Rahab lived and worked in Jericho. Her house, in fact, was built into the thick city wall. She was located in a place and in a profession that enabled her to hear gossip and to assess the thinking of the people. Over the past several months, she had learned enough to know that the people of Jericho, even of the entire land of Canaan, were terrified of a man named Joshua and his army of followers. They had heard about Joshua's God and how he had dried up the Red Sea so that the Israelites could leave Egypt. This God was a mighty God, and Joshua's men were God's men. What would these men do to Jericho?

One night two spies from Joshua's camp arrived in Jericho. To avoid suspicion, they took lodging in Rahab's place of business. But Rahab knew immediately who they were and what they were about. In her mind she weighed the evidence — reports of Joshua's strength and of the power of his God, against the limited preparations of the people of Jericho, plus her love and concern for her own family — and she made a decision. Rahab would protect Joshua's spies and become a spy herself.

During the night, the king of Jericho got word that there were spies in his city and that they were very likely the two strangers lodging at Rahab's house. He sent word to Rahab: "The men in your house have come to spy out the whole country! Bring them out!"

"Some men did come to my house," she answered, "but I don't know where they were from. They left at sundown before the city gate was closed. I didn't find out where they were going, but if you start after them quickly, you can catch them."

The truth was, Rahab had already hidden the spies. They were under some stalks of flax on her roof!

So the King's men, following Rahab's false lead, left the city in search of the spies, and Rahab went up to the roof to get a few things straight. She wanted protection, as she had given protection, not only for herself but for her entire family — a very large family. She told the spies how much the people were frightened. She also told them that she truly believed in their God.

One of the spies said, "If you do not tell anyone what we have been doing, we promise you that when the Lord gives us this land, we will treat you well."

They told her that when the invasion came, she should gather all of her family into her house, that they would not be responsible for anyone left outside. And, she was to tie a red cord to her window, which would be a signal to the invaders. No one in that house would be harmed.

When Joshua's army finally arrived, Rahab did exactly as she had been instructed. Quickly, she rounded up her family — mother, father, brothers, sisters, and all their families. Then she tied a red cord to her window, making sure it was in plain sight. It was a good thing she did this, for the walls of Jericho collapsed and the city was burned to the ground! Rahab and her family, however, had been taken to safety near the Israelite camp. In this way she was rewarded for her

service to God. Rahab, God's spy, and her descendants continued to live in Israel from that day forward.

What is this story *really* about?

Service:

God uses all kinds of people in his service. He used
Rahab, who was a prostitute. Why did he choose her? What
was her motive for serving God? Was it a good motive or a weak
one? Why? Would it be a good motive by today's standards?

Rewards:

Rahab and her entire family were taken to safety, as a
reward for her work as a spy. All of us like to be rewarded when
we do good work. Sometimes it's a raise in pay; sometimes it's a
medal, or a "thank you" letter; sometimes a smile or a hug is
enough reward. There are times, though, when rewards never
come, and we feel cheated.

Let's *talk* about it!

Everyone has heard of the great prophets — Moses, Elijah, Isaiah, Jeremiah, and others. Many minor prophets have also enjoyed a bit of fame over the years, including Hosea, Joel, Malachi, and Zechariah. Those are wonderful names, but where are the women? Where are the prophets with names like Miriam, Anna, Liz . . . or Debbie?

Guess what? Those women really were prophets. Even Liz and Debbie, though it's doubtful anyone ever called them that. Who would have dared!

Deborah was a prophet, inspired by God. She was also a Hebrew judge, by consent of the common people, an honor given to no other woman mentioned in the Bible. Her courthouse was the shade of a palm tree in the open hill country, and her clients were the people of Ephriam, who would go to her at the "tree of Deborah" and wait in line for her decisions. She was intelligent, courageous, faithful, and highly respected.

Deborah's greatest achievement, however, was uniting the scattered tribes of Israel in a common loyalty to God. This religious unity proved crucial to the nation of Israel, and Deborah's part in it earned her the title, "Mother of Israel."

This is how she did it:

One day, as prophet, not judge, she sent for a man named Barak and told him what the Lord intended him to do. She prophesied, "The Lord God of Israel has commanded you to lead ten thousand men into battle against Sisera, the Canaanite," she said. "He has promised you victory."

This was a formidable task, but Barak had faith in Deborah's communion with God. He was willing, but he added a condition.

"I'll go, if you go with me," he said.

35

Deborah considered this, then answered, "All right, I'll go with you, but you won't get credit for the victory. The Lord will hand Sisera over to a woman!"

Strangely enough, she wasn't referring to herself.

Well, Deborah and Barak talked with the leaders of several tribes — Ephriam, Benjamin, Zebulun, Issachar, Machir, Naphtali — and convinced them to go to the Kishon River to fight Sisera in the name of the Lord.

Their strategy was a good old surprise attack, rushing down on the enemy from Mount Tabor. Sisera and all his men in their fancy chariots were thoroughly confused! Barak was able to conquer them to the last man — except for Sisera himself. The commander had fled on foot to a tent in the hills.

Sisera, relaxing in the tent, thought he was in friendly hands, but the hands — those of a woman — only looked friendly. Her name was Jael.

Meantime, Barak looked all over for Sisera. He knew the commander had escaped. He searched the riverbanks, the valley, the hills, and, finally, he arrived at Jael's tent.

"Come here!" Jael said. "I'll show you the man you're looking for."

When Barak entered the tent, he found Sisera, the great Canaanite commander, dead. . . . Friendly Jael had killed him with a tent peg. This was the woman Deborah had spoken about. This was the woman she said would get credit for the victory.

Of course, God received the real and full credit. Everyone knew that. And everyone celebrated. The highlight of that celebration was a song of praise to God, sung by the leaders of the battle, Deborah and Barak. It is the first duet recorded in the Bible. Its words are memorable:

> Listen, you kings!
> Pay attention, you rulers!
> I will sing and play music
> to Israel's God, the Lord. . . .

Tell of it, you that ride on white donkeys,
   sitting on saddles,
and you that must walk wherever you go.
Listen! The noisy crowds around the wells
   are telling of the Lord's victories,
   the victories of Israel's people! . . .
So may all your enemies die like that,
   O Lord,
But may your friends shine
   like the rising sun!

After Deborah's triumph, there was peace in the land for forty years.

She was a prophet, a judge, a powerful, wonderful woman. She was the "Mother of Israel." . . . and I wouldn't dream of calling her Debbie!

What is this story *really* about?

Unity:

There is strength in unity, whether it be in armies, churches, community groups, states, or families. People pulling together get things done. Do you know of churches that are split or fragmented? What has happened to them? What happens to church groups or classes that fragment? How can we build unity in our churches? In our families?

Strength:

Deborah was strong. She was a leader and a judge. The Bible gives us many examples of strong women with leadership qualities. It also gives us examples of "womanly virtues" that include submissiveness. How do you feel about a "woman's place?"

Let's *talk* about it!

Jonathan and David were best friends. They were also brothers-in-law, for David was married to Jonathan's sister.

As in many families, David worked for his father-in-law. He was an officer in King Saul's army, and everyone was proud of him. Every time Saul sent David on a mission, he was successful, and, of course, there was that time earlier, when David had killed Goliath, the giant. The young man was a hero!

What better way to welcome a hero home from battle than with a parade! David had his share of parades, but one parade was especially memorable because the women sang loudly, "Saul has killed thousands, but David tens of thousands!"

This didn't set too well with Saul. He was jealous. He was also worried that David would capture his throne and his kingdom, which should one day belong to Jonathan. Saul had even more reason to fear David — he knew that the Lord was with him!

So what does a jealous, fearful king do about someone who upsets him so? He orders that someone killed, of course. David heard about it and told Jonathan, his best friend.

"My father wants to kill you?" Jonathan was stunned. "David, you can't be serious! If he were planning such a thing, he would have told me. He always tells me his plans, even the smallest ones."

"He's not telling you about this one, because he knows we are friends. He knows it would hurt you."

"Of course it would hurt me! How could I stand to lose my best friend? . . . Are you sure about this, David?"

"I'm sure."

"How can I be sure?" Jonathan asked.

David outlined a plan. "Tomorrow is the New Moon

Festival," he said, "and I am supposed to eat with the king. Instead, I'll go and hide in the field. Tell your father that I'm visiting family in Bethlehem. If he says that's fine, we'll know I'm safe, but if he gets angry, we'll know that he intends to harm me."

"I certainly hope you're wrong," Jonathan answered. "I won't be able to meet you alone after the feast," he continued, "but I will go to the edge of the forest and shoot three arrows toward the rock pile as if it were a target. When the lad who fetches for me runs to pick them up, I'll call out to him. If I say, 'They're on this side,' you'll know you can return home; but, if I say 'they're beyond the pile,' you'll know you must leave at once." Jonathan put his hands on David's shoulders. "If that happens," he said, sadly, "I'll never see you again. . . . Please remember me during my lifetime and also my children after I am gone. . . . Swear to it, David."

David agreed, saying, "The Lord is our witness."

Well, David missed the feast and the king was furious. "Bring him here so that I can kill him!" he shouted.

"But why?" asked Jonathan. "What has he done?"

"As long as David lives," the king answered, "you can never be king."

Jonathan couldn't believe what he was hearing his father say! Saul was speaking of Jonathan's best friend, his daughter's husband — his own son-in-law! And he punctuated his anger by tossing his spear toward Jonathan.

Next day Jonathan went to the forest feeling hurt and ashamed. He quickly shot three arrows toward the rock pile and called out to his servant, "They're beyond the pile!" That was David's signal to leave, but Jonathan made a pretense of lacing his sandal while he sent his servant-boy home. He wanted — needed — to see David one last time . . . to say good-by.

"I'm sorry," he cried, embracing his best friend, "so very sorry! . . . I'll never forget you. Never. . . . And remember, we have put ourselves and our children into God's hands forever."

Jonathan saw David only one time after that. Later, David became king.

Later still, after Jonathan died in battle, David located Jonathan's only son — a crippled young man — and took him into his own home to live.

What is this story *really* about?

Friendship:

David's and Jonathan's friendship was a true bond of brotherly love — not the kind of love that blinds, but the kind that opens eyes. Both young men had their eyes opened to jealousy and cruelty. How did they react? How did this "awakening" affect their friendship? Should best friends always be best friends "no matter what"? What might sever a bonding friendship? Why?

Jealousy:

King Saul was jealous. How is jealousy harmful to relationships? How can it hurt the person who is jealous? Think about some ways to control jealousy. Is jealousy ever good?

Loyalty:

Jonathan was loyal to David — he helped him get away. David was loyal to Jonathan — he took care of Jonathan's son, as he had promised. What does loyalty mean to you?

Let's *talk* about it!

(The story of Jonathan and David is adapted from *"Five Men Touched by God"* by Janet Litherland. Copyright © 1978, Meriwether Publishing Inc.)

The Queen of Sheba
(I Kings 10:1-13)

"Who do you think you are — the Queen of Sheba?" My mother asked me that once with a smile on her face, when I was a child dressed in discarded finery, too-big high heels, and pop-it beads.

I had heard of the Queen of England, and of the Queen of Hearts who baked some tarts, but who in the world was the Queen of Sheba? Or was that just a name Mother had made up?

I didn't ask questions at the time, but later, when I grew up and studied parts of the Old Testament in Sunday School, I was surprised to find that the Queen of Sheba had been a real live lady in King Solomon's time.

"Who do you think you are — the Queen of Sheba?" It was an appropriate comparison. This was a queen who loved to dress up in fine clothing and dazzling jewels. She had plenty of wealth to do it with, too. Her country, Sheba, was a center of trade for a large area, and her people specialized in trading precious stones and spices. They also liked gold.

One day the Queen of Sheba heard about King Solomon and all his riches. She also heard that he was the smartest ruler anyone knew of. He knew how and what to order his people to do so that everyone would reap maximum benefits. People speculated that this was why he was so rich.

The queen decided to see for herelf. She arranged a visit with King Solomon, which was no easy task, because she had to travel a great distance with a great deal of luggage. Believe me, this Queen of Sheba did not travel lightly! She took a large group of servants with her as well as camels loaded with gifts for the king. What kind of gifts? . . . The kind that were most available to her, of course — precious jewels, spices, and gold. She may have overdone it a little with the gold. She packed nearly five tons!

Solomon was impressed. Of course the reason for her visit, so she said, was to test his wisdom. He thought that might be a fun way to spend an evening, so they sat down to some sporting conversation. People in those days really enjoyed a good game of wits. She asked a lot of hard questions — everything she could think of — and he answered every one of them. Nothing was too difficult for him to explain. He was even smarter than the queen had expected!

When they finished their game, King Solomon took her on a tour of the palace. She was amazed at the splendor of his living quarters and those of his officials, the efficient organization of his staff and their elegant uniforms, the food that was served, and even the sacrifices Solomon offered in the Temple. She took special note of the musicians and their magnificent instruments — harps and lyres made of imported juniper wood. The wood was like pine but whiter, and it had more sheen. She had never seen anything like it. Solomon's palace left her breathless!

"I did not believe what they told me until I came and saw for myself," she said. "You are even wiser than people say." Then she praised God for giving Israel such a wise king.

Before she left to return to her country, Solomon gave her many gifts to take back with her. He was also wise, you see, in the area of economics!

"Who do you think you are — the Queen of Sheba?"

Yes, indeed!

What is this story *really* about?

Curiosity:

Have you ever been so curious about something that you almost couldn't stand it until you knew? Were you able to control your curiosity? The Queen of Sheba just had to discover Solomon's wisdom for herself. Would you be comfortable doing something like that? Children are curious creatures — it's charming. What is the difference between being curious and being just plain nosy?

Negotiation:

Negotiation in Bible times involved a lot of conversation — back and forth, back and forth, like a game. Is it any different today? Or do we quickly "cut to the bottom line"? Too quickly? What is the value in negotiation?

Let's *talk* about it!

Elisha was a friend of the great prophet and miracle-worker, Elijah. He was a witness when Elijah was taken dramatically to heaven in a chariot of fire, and he became Elijah's successor on earth. He inherited Elijah's band of prophets, his responsibilities, and even the power to perform miracles, as Elijah had done. Elisha's miracles were especially colorful:

The Parting of the Jordan River (2:14)

Of course you've heard of the parting of the Red Sea by Moses, but did you know that Elisha parted the waters of the Jordan River? It was his first miracle, and it happened by accident. Elijah had done the same thing just moments before, but Elijah was dead now, and Elisha was grief-stricken. He pulled off his coat, ripped it, and cast it aside. Then he picked up Elijah's coat, which had been left behind. For a few moments he stood on the bank of the Jordan River, clutching Elijah's coat and thinking of the friend he would never see again.

Suddenly, he struck the water with Elijah's coat and demanded, "Where is the Lord, the God of Elijah?"

He struck the water again. This time it divided, and he was able to walk across to the other side! There were fifty prophets over there who saw Elisha do this, and they were quick to recognize him as their new leader.

The Amazing Olive Oil (4:1-7)

One day Elisha was approached by a woman whose husband had recently died. She was worried because a debt-collector had come and she had no money to pay the debt her late husband had left. As payment, the collector was insisting that she hand over her two sons as slaves. She was sure that Elisha could help her.

Elisha asked what she had at home that she might sell.

44

She thought a moment and replied, "Only a small jar of olive oil."

"Go to your neighbors and borrow as many empty jars as you can," Elisha told her. "Then you and your sons go into the house, close the door, and start pouring oil into the jars. Set each one aside as soon as it is full."

The woman and her sons did this, watching in amazement as oil continued to flow from their one small jar. When all of the borrowed containers were full, the family was able to sell the oil for enough money to pay off the debt. They even had money left over to live on!

Twenty Loaves for One Hundred Men (4:42-44)

Elisha had one hundred hungry prophets on his hands and no food to give them. When a stranger appeared with twenty barley loaves and some fresh ears of grain, Elisha knew that his men would no longer be hungry.

His servant wasn't so sure. "Do you think this is enough for a hundred men?" he asked.

We know, of course, that Jesus divided five loaves and two fish among five thousand people, but did the prophet Elisha perform the same miracle eight hundred years earlier?

He certainly did! The loaves and grain were given to the men, and there was enough for everyone to eat. Like the miracle of the olive oil, there was plenty left over!

The Floating Ax Head (6:1-7)

One day Elisha and his prophets went to the woods alongside the Jordan River to cut down some trees. They had outgrown the house they were living in, and they were building a new, larger one.

As one of the men was felling a tree, his ax head suddenly popped off its handle and fell in the river. He was really upset, not so much that he had lost an ax head, but that he had lost a borrowed ax head. How would he ever explain it or replace it?

"Where did it fall?" Elisha asked.

The man showed him the place. Elisha cut off a stick, threw it in the water, and made the ax head float!

What a wonderful miracle! The man was able to reach into the water, lift out the precious ax head, and get back to work.

Elisha's Last Miracle (13:14-19)

As Elisha lay dying, King Jehoash of Israel rushed to visit him. The king was overcome with grief, because he had looked upon Elisha as a father, the mighty defender of Israel.

Elisha decided that he would help the king, even though he himself was bedridden. He told him to get a bow and some arrows and to shoot one of the arrows through Elisha's open window.

When he had done this, Elisha said, "You are the Lord's arrow with which he will win victory over Syria." He then told the king to strike the ground with the remaining arrows.

The king picked up the arrows and hit the ground three times. But this did not please Elisha.

"You should have struck five or six times," he said, "and then you would have won complete victory over the Syrians; but now you will defeat them only three times."

That was the bad news. The good news is this: Jehoash's son, Jeroboam II, managed to recover all of the cities that Syria had taken from Israel over the years!

Elisha's Very Last Miracle (13:21)

For years after Elisha's death, bands of Moabites continued to invade Israel's land, like pesky swarms of beetles, frightening the people of the small communities. One day, when a family of Israelites was having a funeral for one of their own, a band of Moabites came to scare them. The frightened people quickly threw their corpse into Elisha's tomb and ran off. As soon as the body came into contact with Elisha's bones, the man came back to life and stood up.

Who do you think was scared then?

Elisha was a beloved leader of the biblical prophets. Because of this, stories of his greatness have been lovingly preserved, told, and retold across many centuries. Everything

Elisha did, even his "little" miracles, he did in the name of the Lord.

What is this story *really* about?

Greatness:

Elisha was a friend of the great prophet Elijah. Elisha became great himself. What was special about him? A person doesn't have to be a miracle-worker to be great. Think of some public figures today whom you consider to have achieved greatness. How did they do it?

Faith:

Miracles happen because of faith. Elisha knew that whatever he did in the name of the Lord would work. Is that a special kind of faith, or is that just the way it is? If we have faith, can we be sure that God will answer our prayers?

Let's *talk* about it!

JOSIAH'S PROMISE
(II Chronicles 34)

Everyone knows what it means to make a promise. Everyone also knows what it means to break a promise. Some people break them as easily as they make them, but, for most of us, a promise is like a vow — it is important.

Lots of promises are recorded in the scriptures, especially in the Old Testament, but one promise stands out from the others because it caused a great change in the people of Judah. It was made by a young man just twenty-six years old. His name was Josiah, and he was a king.

Do you think twenty-six is young for a king? Actually, Josiah had already been king for eighteen years! When a child is put in a position of such enormous responsibility, he or she has little choice but to grow up fast.

When Josiah became king, at age eight, the people of Judah did not worship the God of Israel. They worshiped idols or images, the sun, moon, stars, and the planets. They dabbled in astrology and in the occult. Josiah didn't particularly like all of this, but he wasn't strongly motivated to do anything about it until, at age sixteen, he overcame the influence of idolatry and chose to follow the God of David — the Lord God of Israel. Four years later, at age twenty, he started taking action against idolatry. Priests who had served former kings were removed from office, but Josiah, because he was a kind ruler, made provisions for their support. He then had the idols destroyed and the pagan places of worship smashed and burned, not just in Jerusalem but all over Judah. Finally, King Josiah ordered the restoration of the Temple at Jerusalem.

It was during the restoration that a workman found something terribly important — Moses' Book of the Law, which had been lost and forgotten for nearly one hundred and fifty years! Just imagine how you'd feel if you were repairing a wall in your kitchen and you found a book or a letter that had been hidden there for many years. That would be exciting! Carefully, the precious treasure was lifted from its hiding place and taken to King Josiah.

"Please read it to me," he said. "All of it."

And he settled back and listened to the most astounding words he had ever heard. He knew they were the words of the Lord, and he also knew that those words had not been obeyed by the people of Judah. . . . The Lord's people. This upset him so badly that he wept and humbled himself before God.

Then he turned to his attendants. "The Lord must be very angry," he cried. "Go! Consult with a prophet. Find out about the teachings of this book!"

The attendants hurried to find Huldah the prophetess, who lived in the newer part of Jerusalem. When they told her about the book, she gave them this message from the Lord:

"I am going to punish Jerusalem and all its people with the curses written in the book that was read to the king. They have rejected me and have offered sacrifices to other gods, and so have stirred up my anger by all they have done. My anger is aroused against Jerusalem, and it will not die down. As for the king himself, this is what I, the Lord God of Israel, say: You listened to what is written in the book, and you repented and humbled yourself before me, tearing your clothes and weeping, when you heard how I threatened to punish Jerusalem and its people. I have heard your prayer, and the punishment which I am going to bring on Jerusalem will not come until after your death. I will let you die in peace."

The men returned to King Josiah with the message.

This, now, is where Josiah's promise comes in. He summoned all of the leaders, the priests, the Levites, and all other people, rich and poor, to meet him at the Temple. There he read to them the entire Book of the Law, as it had been read to him.

When he had finished, he said to the Lord, "I promise to obey you, to keep your laws and commands with all my heart and soul, and to put into practice the demands attached to this

49

promise, as written in the book." He also made all the people promise the same thing.

King Josiah — this young man — became an outstanding ruler with good political and religious control over his country. At age thirty-nine he was killed in battle and buried in Jerusalem, where all of Judah mourned his passing.

Because of his promise, and the fact that he kept it, there was one last important surge of religious revival before the fall of Jerusalem.

Young Josiah was one of Judah's greatest kings.

What is this story *really* about?

Promises:

Josiah not only made a promise to God, he kept it. Keeping promises is a sign of dependability. God could and did depend on Josiah. Have you ever broken a promise? Why? Is there a good reason for breaking one? How do you feel when you're the victim of a broken promise?

Youth:

Josiah was young for a king, but that didn't seem to be a disadvantage. He became one of Judah's greatest kings. Read I Timothy 4:12-16. It has some interesting things to say about being young.

Responsibility:

Some people learn responsibility at an early age. Others never learn it. What factors might make a person irresponsible?

Let's *talk* about it!

THE DETHRONEMENT OF VASHTI
(Esther 1)

This is the story of a queen whose royal status was taken away from her for no good reason. By today's standards of right and wrong, and decency and equality, the story seems incredible.

The queen's name was Vashti, which in Hebrew means "beautiful woman," and we must assume that she was truly beautiful. She was married to Xerxes I, King of Persia. In those days Persia included one hundred and twenty-seven provinces from India to Ethiopia to Greece — an enormous chunk of land, which made Xerxes a powerful and important king.

During the third year of his reign, King Xerxes acted upon a whim. He devoted six whole months to showing everyone — and that means everyone — just how important he was. He invited all of the governors and noblemen of his provinces, as well as his elite bodyguard — the "Ten Thousand Immortals," he called them — to his palace for parties and feasting, and tours of the majestic royal grounds. He loved showing off his riches.

But the guest list wasn't long enough to satisfy him. Xerxes decided it would be even more fun to impress the common people. So he arranged for a banquet to be held in the gardens of the royal palace. The guest list would include everyone in the captial city of Susa, rich people and poor people. No one would be left out.

Now, if you and I were to give a big party, we might expect it to last several hours. Well, Xerxes' party lasted several days! Seven, to be exact. And he didn't just decorate tables. The courtyard was hung with curtains made of fine fabric. The fabric was tied with royal purple cords to silver rings, which were attached to the huge marble pillars around the area. Furniture made of gold and silver was strategically placed on the mosaic paving, so that everyone would look down and notice the beauty beneath their feet — white marble, red feldspar, blue turquoise, and sparkling mother-of-pearl. It is interesting to know that archeological remains of the very same marble pillars and mosaic paving exist to the present day. They are approximately two thousand, five hundred years old!

For our banquet, we might bring out our best china and silver, if we had any, but Xerxes brought out one-of-a-kind real gold cups. His servants filled them with royal wine, and there was no limit to the amount a guest could drink. Everything was "on the house," of course.

Because there were so many guests, this enormous banquet was divided into two units: While King Xerxes entertained the men in the gardens, Queen Vashti entertained the women in magnificent rooms inside the palace.

On the seventh day of the banquet, the king, who was quite drunk and a little obnoxious by this time, ordered his servants to bring Queen Vashti to the men's banquet. He wanted to show off his most prized possession, his beautiful wife, certainly the envy of every man at the party.

"Tell her to wear her royal crown," he ordered.

Early Jewish scholars reported that the crown was all Xerxes wanted Vashti to wear! At any rate, she refused to appear before him and his drunken friends, and this made Xerxes furious.

So he summoned his council and asked their opinion, which was the custom, since they were responsible for matters involving law and order.

"I, King Xerxes, sent my servants to Queen Vashti with a command, and she refused to obey it!" he thundered. "What does the law say that we should do with her?"

Memucan, one of the officials answered, "Queen Vashti has insulted not only the king but also his officials — in fact, every man in the empire! Every woman in the empire will start looking down on her husband as soon as she hears what the queen has done. . . . Wives everywhere will have no respect for their husbands, and husbands will be angry with their wives."

"What do you suggest?' asked the king.

"If it please your majesty, issue a royal proclamation that Vashti may never again appear before the king."

In other words — divorce her! For refusing to exhibit herself to all the men of Susa in her birthday suit!

But take it a step further, Memucan suggested. Write it into Persian law so it cannot be revoked. Make the divorce final. Make an example of Vashti. Show her who is boss! "When this is done," he said, "every woman will treat her husband with proper respect."

The king and his officials liked this idea . . . and it was done. In addition, the king sent a message to each of his royal provinces, saying that every husband should be the master of his home and speak with final authority.

Sometime later, when Xerxes had sobered up, he regretted what he had done to his beautiful wife. . . . But it was too late.

What is this story *really* about?

Showing Off:

Xerxes was a show-off. He liked to impress people with his wealth, his palace, his servants, even his wife. Do you know people like that? Do they impress you, as they intend to do? Why or why not? How do you handle show-offs without alienating them?

Manipulation:

Xerxes tried to manipulate Vashti. He used a threat, then had to make good on it. In a sense he intended to use her to feed his own ego. Do you know anyone who manipulates other people for personal gain? Why don't folks "catch on" to their manipulators? How can we keep ourselves from becoming victims?

Personal Pride:

Vashti had personal pride. She refused to be an object for exhibition. We hear much about pride being dangerous and about its "going before a fall," but there are times when pride is a good thing.

Regret:

Xerxes regretted what he had done, but it was too late. We all have regrets that need to be dealt with. In Philippians, Paul speaks of being less than perfect, but, he says, ". . .the one thing I do, however, is to forget what is behind me and do my best to reach what is ahead." (Philippians 3:13) Past regrets can shape our futures in a positive way if we learn from our mistakes.

Let's *talk* about it!

Job was a perfect person — at least he thought he was. He was a rich man. He had great herds of cattle, sheep, camels, and donkeys. He had a big house and, of course, many servants to take care of everything. He was also a good, family man who worshiped God and stayed out of trouble. Even God was impressed with Job's goodness.

"Did you notice my servant Job?" the Lord asked Satan one day. "There is no one on earth as faithful and good as he is. He worships me and is careful not to do anything evil."

"That's because you protect him all the time," Satan replied. "I'll bet if you take away everything he has, he won't be such a faithful goody-goody."

Would Job remain faithful? . . . The Lord decided to accept that challenge. So he turned Job, his family, and his possessions over to Satan on one condition: "You must not hurt Job himself."

Well, Satan had always loved making a mess of things, so he went into Job's situation with great glee. But what was wonderful for Satan turned out to be tragic for Job. Job suddenly found himself facing the worst disaster of his life. Make that *many* disasters!

First, lightning killed his sheep. Then bandits stole his oxen. Raiders drove off his camels and killed his servants. And, if that weren't enough, a terrible storm destroyed the house of Job's oldest son with all of Job's children inside. None survived.

Job was overcome with grief, but, remarkably, he did not blame God.

Did not blame God? Satan was not happy. He didn't like being a loser.

Next thing Job knew, there were sores breaking out all over his body. He was stricken with a disease so horrible that he went to sit among the howling dogs near the garbage dump, feeling much like garbage himself. He was homeless, childless, penniless; and now his body, too, was worthless.

Still, he did not blame God. He said, "When God sends us something good, we welcome it. How can we complain when he sends us trouble?" (What he didn't know was that the trouble had come from Satan, not God.)

While Job was sitting by the garbage dump, grieving for his family, his possessions, and for himself, three of his friends came to visit. They hardly recognized him as the handsome, confident man they had known. He was scratching his sores and moaning with pain and despair. The friends were so overwhelmed by his condition that they couldn't speak at first. Instead, they simply sat with him and kept him company. They were such good friends that they sat for an entire week without talking!

Finally, Job broke the silence. He cried, "I wish I had never been born!" . . . Then he sobbed, "Why me? . . . Why has all of this happened to me?"

Well, his good friends decided it was time for good advice. One at a time they gave it to him.

The first, Eliphaz, was kind and considerate. He tried the pious approach: Seek God, repent of your sins, and everything will be fine.

The second friend, Bildad, was a little sharp-tongued. He came right out and said that sin gets punished and that justice was being done.

The third, Zophar, thought himself a direct and honest person, so he advised Job to give up trying to understand God. To him it was a waste of time.

"Don't you three know anything at all?" Job cried. "I am innocent! I am a good man, not a sinner! God is testing me. Your words don't apply."

"We're just trying to help," they replied.

"Then listen to what I am saying. I am a righteous man. I know God. And I can hold my head high in his presence."

His friends didn't know what to do with him. But there was a young man nearby who had been listening all the time. His name was Elihu, and he had been holding his tongue out of respect for the older ones. Now, however, he was angry and decided to speak his mind, as young people often do. He was angry with Job for justifying himself, and he was angry with Job's friends for giving tidy little answers that solved nothing.

"Listen, Job," said Elihu. "You have said that you are righteous and that God is testing you. Well, I say you failed the test."

"What? I failed!"

"Yes, failed. You are guilty of proclaiming your righteousness. Do you help God by being so righteous? There is nothing God needs from you."

He went on to explain that God saves people every day from words and thoughts, or from unkind things they do — from things they aren't even aware of! "God is all-powerful, and, best of all, merciful," he said.

Suddenly, lightning struck with a loud clap! . . . Everything got quiet. . . . and out of the quietness came . . . yes, the Voice of God!

"Who are you, Job, to question my wisdom with your ignorant, empty words?" the Lord asked. "Stand up now like a man and answer the questions I ask you." Job stood up in a hurry.

God didn't have just a few questions — he had fifty of them! Things like, "Were you there when I made the world? . . . Have you walked on the floor of the ocean? . . . Does either the rain or the dew have a father? . . . Can you guide the stars season by season? . . . Does an eagle wait for your command?"

Job felt foolish. He had no answers. He sat down.

But the Lord put on more pressure. "Stand up now like a man and answer my questions," he repeated. Job stood, and the Lord went on with sixteen more of them!

Finally, Job answered (without sitting down!), "I know, Lord, that you are all-powerful; that you can do everything you want. You ask how I dare question your wisdom when I am so very ignorant. I talked about things I did not understand, about marvels too great for me to know. You told me to listen while you spoke and to try to answer your questions. In the past I knew only what others had told me, but now I have seen you with my own eyes. So I am ashamed of all I have said and repent in dust and ashes."

That was the right answer.

You know what the Lord did then? He blessed Job with twice as much as he had in the beginning. He gave him fourteen thousand sheep, six thousand camels, two thousand head of cattle, one thousand donkeys, seven more sons and three more daughters.

Job, still a good man but now a humble man, was a wealthy man once again. He was also a healthy man — he lived for one hundred and forty more years!

What is this story *really* about?

Righteousness:

A righteous person always strives to do what is "right." If righteousness becomes a person's total focus, that person is said to be "self-righteous," a derogatory term. Job was a righteous man. Even the Lord said so. He wasn't "self-righteous," because his focus was on God; however, he had a problem admitting his own sin. If a person always does right, how can he do wrong? That was Job's dilemma. Think about it.

Faithfulness:

Job was rewarded not for his righteousness but for his faithfulness. Satan despises faithfulness to God. Have you ever thought that the harder you try to be faithful, the harder it gets? Why do you suppose that is?

Humility:

Humility is a difficult thing to achieve in our high-tech world. We're smart, sophisticated, and self-confident — all admirable traits. Yet humility is the only thing that moves a Christian from a formal to a personal knowledge of God.

Let's *talk* about it!

LITTLE CREATURES DO BIG THINGS
(Proverbs 30:24-28)

There are four animals in the world that are small, but very, very clever:

Ants are tiny and weak, but they work hard and stay busy. They have bosses, called queens, who keep things organized. Even their homes are organized. They don't have a living room, a bedroom, and a kitchen like we do, but their underground chambers are divided into nurseries, granaries, and fungus gardens, all of which they use to prepare and store food for winter. One type of ant, the harvester, takes wet grain from the granary to the surface on sunny days and spreads it out to dry. Most ants like to eat sweet things, so watch your doughnuts!

Rock badgers look sort of like a cross between a rabbit and a rat, maybe like a guinea pig. They live and hide in the rocks of mountain ranges, and they love to stretch out on those rocks and sun themselves. This gives them a vantage point for spotting enemies. Like the ants, rock badgers are very industrious. They gather flowers, leaves, and stems and arrange them in neat little haystacks among the rocks, where they'll be shelterd from the rain. This is their winter food supply. Some of those stacks contain as much as a bushel of food!

Locusts are the uncles and cousins of grasshoppers. They don't have a leader, as the ants do, but somehow they manage to move in formation without changing direction or bumping into one another. They either march like an army or fly in bands, like an air force. They are powerful and determined. And, once they get focused on something, they are unstoppable!

Lizards are related to crocodiles and even dinosaurs, but they are miniature in comparison, small enough to hold in your hand. Their scaly little bodies with four legs can grip any surface — they can walk straight up a wall without falling off!

They have long tapered tails, which on some lizards are detachable. That way, if an enemy grabs one by the tail, the lizard simply breaks off his tail and runs. They're quick, too. Some even travel up to fifteen miles per hour. Imagine how easy it would be for such a clever little creature to get into places where you'd least expect to find him. Why, lizards can even sneak into kings' palaces!

Ants, rock badgers, locusts, and lizards are small. They're also smart and busy. They're organized, they make plans, and they follow through. Maybe they also teach . . . without even knowing it!

NOTE: This little story is tailor-made for props. Use pictures or drawings of each animal and sing the hymn, "All Things Bright and Beautiful, All Creatures Great and Small," found in most hymnals.

What is this story *really* about?

Organization:

Have you ever found that the more you have to do, the less you get done? There's an old saying, "If you need something done, ask a busy person to do it." It's not that a busy person has more time, it's that he or she is organized. How can we help ourselves and our families make better use of our time and talents?

Productivity:

Good organization leads to productivity. We should produce daily for the Lord. What does this mean? How can we do it? How can we measure Christian productivity?

Size:

Little creatures do big things. So do little people. We're not referring to "short" people here, but to all of us who feel small in a huge world. We can make a difference, if not individually, then certainly collectively — as Christians, working together for God.

Let's *talk* about it!

LIFE ISN'T FAIR
(Book of Ecclesiastes)

There are people in this world who claim to know many things. They are said to be wise, or extra smart. They may be called geniuses or, if they're young, "whiz kids." Not all of these extra smart people, however, are truly great thinkers. It takes a special kind of person to dig really deep into the issues that bother all of us and pull them up into the sunshine where they can be examined. This kind of thinking is risky. It exposes not only the issues but the person who is examining them. He or she bares his or her mind for everyone to see.

One such person lived many hundreds of years ago. His ideas were so popular in his day that they were preserved and later canonized as part of our Old Testament, even though they now seem contrary to what we consider "properly religious."

"Life is useless," the Thinker cries. "What has been done before will be done again." He sees God as the Creator, not as a personal Redeemer — not exactly what we expect to find in the Bible. . . . But it does make us think.

This man who makes us think calls himself Koheleth, a Hebrew name, which translates as "The Philosopher," or, as many have come to call him, "The Preacher." He talks to us through the Book of Ecclesiastes.

We know that Koheleth was a professional teacher with deep faith, but to call him a preacher is a little misleading. His teachings were not about God; they were about life, and his view of life was that it is too short. Therefore, it should be lived to the fullest.

To imagine this extraordinary man, think of someone who is sincere and honest, but who is moody and says things that reflect his moods; someone who is able to see both sides of an issue, and who loves to ask questions and demand answers. Picture someone who is kind, but a little . . . well, picky.

All of us have heard things like: "A watched pot never boils," "Necessity is the mother of invention," and "What goes up must come down." These sayings are called maxims, and they have come to us through our parents and grandparents and their parents before them. Our friend, Koheleth, loved maxims, especially ones with deep meaning and humor. He wrote many sayings of his own, and he collected many from the Book of Proverbs. Those he collected, however, he wasn't satisfied with. He felt that the writers hadn't put enough thought into them.

"I decided," he says, "that I would examine and study all the things that are done in the world." Big job! So he criticized and dissected, analyzed and wrote, and re-wrote. He particularly loved to pick at the Proverbs!

For example, one Proverb says that a house is built with wisdom. Koheleth says that a little money helps, too: "Wisdom is good with an inheritance." The Proverbs state over and over that one must work to acquire wisdom, but Koheleth believes that wisdom is a gift of God. We have it or we don't.

Koheleth gives us many of his original maxims, too. Imagine him standing tall and straight, turning suddenly to point his long finger at you and saying, "The more you talk, the more likely you are to say something foolish." Or, "A good reputation is better than expensive perfume." Or, "If you take a bribe, you ruin your character." I like this one: "Patience is better than pride."

But Koheleth is much more than the sum of his witty sayings. He is what we call a "realist." He is sincerely trying to offer help to those of us who find life difficult. Life is not black or white, he says, but many shades of gray. And life isn't fair.

This seems to be his theme — that the world is full of injustice. Some of us work hard all of our lives and still never have anything. Some of us keep "turning the other cheek," as the Bible tells us, only to get that side of our face smacked, too. "If you dig a pit," says Koheleth, "you fall in it; if you break through a wall, a snake bites you." . . . So what is a body to do?

Imagine yourself climbing onto his bony lap, like a small child, tugging at his white beard and whining, "Koheleth, life isn't fair."

He looks you straight in the eye and says, "You're right, it isn't. And nothing will change that."

Disappointed? Did you expect him to say something like, "Trust in the Lord and everything will be rosy?"

No, he tucks his finger under your chin and tells you to make the most of what you have. "Don't let anything worry you or cause you pain," he says. "All of us should eat and drink and enjoy what we have worked for. It is God's gift. . . . If you wait until the wind and the weather are just right, you will never plant anything and never harvest anything."

So you climb down from his lap, feeling a little better about things — at least a little more content with your lot in life — and you resolve that you will quit whining.

Finally, as you walk away, you hear Koheleth say under his breath, "God made us plain and simple, but we have made ourselves very complicated."

What is this story *really* about?

Fairness:

Life isn't fair and it never will be. Neither will it be perfect, as long as there are imperfect people. But that doesn't mean we should give up and let the world deteriorate. What can we do to help ourselves and others adjust to life's inequities?

Being Realistic:

Everyone has dreams, and we hope that many of our dreams will come true in our lifetime. Meanwhile, we live in the "real world," and we have to function in it. There is work to be done, services to render, and someone has to take out the garbage.

Let's *talk* about it!

Love begins in the Garden of Eden — "bone of my bones and flesh of my flesh" — and ends in Revelation — "a bride adorned for her husband." In between, it permeates the teachings of Jesus. Nowhere, however, is love more beautifully expressed than in the Song of Songs. Love, after all, is the song of songs. Love transcends time and space and language. . . . It is "heart music." It is something to sing about!

Song of Songs is a book of poetry, and, like any poetry, it should be considered as a whole, not as individual lines to be dissected. This particular poetry is not only about the love of man and woman but about the love of God. Earthly love, to be sure, is a reflection of heavenly love. "If God so loved us, we also ought to love one another." (I John 4:11)

Throughout the Bible, love is symbolized by the marriage bond, a sacrament. In a romantic way, the Song of Songs presents the spiritual and physical emotions upon which marriage is based. It is appropriate. If the language seems extravagant, it is because love itself is extravagant. It is about choosing and being chosen.

In this story the young man is a shepherd, and the love of his life is a beautiful maiden whose skin is tanned from working in the vineyards. Since she cannot be with him in the hills, she speaks to him within her own head and heart.

"Oh, my dearest love," she cries,
"Where will you be tending your flock today?
Where will you be resting?
I wish with all my heart I could be with you!"

But she has memories of the last time she saw him, and those memories sustain her.

"He calls me a rose of Sharon
and a lily among thorns.
He makes no secret of loving me!

64

Compared to other men he is like
an apple tree among the trees of the forest,
offering cool shade and sweet fruit.
He brings me to the banqueting table,
and his banner over me is love."

Naturally, her joyous feelings are reflected in her eyes, her voice, and her step, making her appear more beautiful than ever — radiant! Everyone notices. Even the king himself is attracted to her and tries to court her while her shepherd is away.

The king's method is elaborate. He comes in a cloud of smoke, smelling of myrrh and frankincense; he drives his finest chariot, made from the wood of Lebanon and decorated with silver and gold; he even wears his crown! . . . But the young maiden is not impressed.

"My beloved is the chiefest among ten thousand,"
she says.
"His head is as the most fine gold,
His locks are bushy and black as a raven.
His eyes are as the eyes of doves . . .
His cheeks are as a bed of spices . . .
His hands are as gold rings . . .
His legs are as pillars of marble set upon
sockets of gold . . .
Yea, he is altogether lovely.
This is my beloved!"

What need had she of a king?

Then one day she hears her shepherd's voice:

"Rise up, my love, my fair one,
and come away.
For, lo, the winter is past,
The rain is over and gone.
The flowers appear on the earth,
The time of the singing of birds is come.
Arise, my love, my fair one,
and come away.

Of course she goes to him. And his marriage proposal comes as no surprise:

"Close your heart to every love but mine;
   hold no one in your arms but me.
Love is as powerful as death;
   passion is as strong as death itself.
It bursts into flame
   and burns like a raging fire.
Water cannot put it out;
   no flood can drown it."

She replies, "My beloved is mine and I am his."

Song of Songs is wedding music. Not just beautiful melody, but complete harmony — man, woman, and God!

What is this story *really* about?

Love:

Current Biblical thinking divides love into three categories, based on shadings from the Greek language:

AGAPE — God-filled love, within people
PHILOS — Brotherly love, among family members
EROS — Physical love, between a man and a woman

"Song of Songs" praises the most powerful force in the world. "Love is as strong as death," it says (8:6). That's about as strong as anything can get. And God gave it to us. What do we do with it? Think about the different kinds of love.

Let's *talk* about it!

The next-to-last king of Judah before the fall of Jerusalem and the destruction of the Temple, was an eighteen-year-old boy named Jehoiachin. He had had two kingly examples to follow — his grandfather, Josiah, a good king and a kind man who pleased the Lord and was loved by the people; and his father, Jehoiakim, an oppressive and godless king who cut and burned certain pages of Jeremiah's prophecy because they displeased him. Young Jehoiachin followed his father's example.

According to the prophet Ezekiel, Jehoiachin was like a cub, raised among lions and taught to hunt: "He wrecked forts, he ruined towns. The people of the land were terrified every time he roared." Jeremiah had similar feelings about the young lion, but he and Ezekiel did not necessarily represent the people. Most folks simply said, "boys will be boys." Jehoiachin was their hope for the future. They liked his strength, his decisiveness, and his youth.

His reign, however, lasted only three months and ten days. He had inherited a weak and disintegrating kingdom, thanks to his father, which made it fairly easy for his rival, Nebuchadnezzar, to move in. Nebuchadnezzar's army attacked Jerusalem and took the young king prisoner. The army also took all the royal princes, the men of power, and all skilled workers to exile in Babylonia, leaving only the poorest people behind in Judah. To these people, young Jehoiachin was their legitimate king, and they hoped that one day he would be restored to the throne. . . . He never was.

Jehoiachin remained in prison for thirty-seven years. But then an interesting thing happened. Nebuchadnezzar died and his son, Evilmerodach, became king. For some unexplained reason, Evilmerodach had a kind spot in his heart for Jehoiachin. Though he kept him in exile, he released him from prison and elevated him to a position above the other exiled kings. Evilmerodach exchanged Jehoiachin's prison garments for more kingly attire and invited him to dine at the king's table for the rest of his life. Each day for as long as Jehoiachin lived, he was given a regular allowance for his needs.

What is this story *really* about?

Paying the Price:

Nothing is truly "free." If you want something, you must pay for it. Jehoiachin paid the price (37 years in prison) for his father's reign of oppression and terror. Jesus paid the price (death on a cross) for the sins of the world. Have you ever sacrificed or "paid a price" for something you really wanted or believed in? Was it worth it?

Kindness:

Evilmerodach treated Jehoiachin with kindness even though Jehoiachin was his prisoner. It was not possible to release the prisoner, but it was possible to make his life more pleasant. Kindness is a Christian virtue. It is one of the "Fruits of the Spirit" (Galatians 5:22).

Can you think of everyday unkindnesses that can be avoided? We make excuses for ourselves for a lot of things, but there is no excuse for being unkind.

Let's *talk* about it!

Close your eyes for a moment and think about what it would be like if God suddenly spoke to you — out loud, with real words — and told you to do something scary. . . . Would you do it? Ezekiel did. He was a man who lived in Old Testament times. He was a prophet, which is sort of like a preacher, except that prophets can predict future events. Micah, remember, predicted that a great Ruler would be born in tiny Bethlehem, and it really happened.

Well, God not only spoke to Ezekiel, he picked him up with his spirit and took him to a valley where the ground was covered with bones. This wasn't just any old valley scattered with animal carcasses. It was a deserted battlefield, and the bones were those of human soldiers.

Ezekiel had been there once, a long time before the battle, when the valley was green and beautiful. But that visit was no fun either, because God had taken him there to tell him about terrible things that would happen. God told him that the Israelites, because of all the evil, disgusting things they did (including the worshiping of idols) would die in war or of starvation or disease.

"They will feel all the force of my anger," God had said. "Corpses will be scattered among the idols and around the altars, scattered on every high hill, on the top of every mountain, under every green tree and every large oak, in every place where they burned sacrifices to their idols." That's what God had said.

And here was Ezekiel now, returned to the valley . . . And it was covered with bones — dry, brittle, human bones.

You need to know that bones meant a great deal more to people in the ancient world than they do to us. Those folks believed that a person's soul was contained in his bones. With that thought, imagine Ezekiel's state of mind as he looked out over that valley.

Let's imagine further that it was nearly dark. The sun had gone down and the wind was blowing across that immense graveyard, stirring up dust. Then the Lord said to Ezekiel, "Can these bones come back to life?"

I would have said, "Wait a minute, Lord. Hold it right there! What's dead is dead." I've always been a little skittish in graveyards anyway, particularly at night. And these bones weren't even buried!

If Ezekiel felt that way, he didn't let on. He said, "Come back to life? Lord, only you can answer that." He played it safe.

So the Lord said, "Ezekiel, prophesy to the bones. Tell these dry bones to listen to the word of the Lord. Tell them, 'I am going to put breath into you and bring you back to life. I will give you muscles and cover you with skin.'"

Oh, dear. And now the moon glowed, too. But Ezekiel did as he was told. While he was speaking he heard a rattling noise, and the bones began to join together. . . . You guessed it — the foot bone connected to the . . . leg bone. The leg bone connected to the . . . knee bone. And all "them bones" connected to one another — all the way to the head!

Well, the Bible doesn't say so, but I'll bet Ezekiel's own bones were rattling, too. And as he stood there, his knees shaking and his teeth chattering, the bones of the valley developed muscles, then skin. . . . Things were looking better, but still there was no breath.

God said to Ezekiel, "Tell the wind that the Sovereign Lord commands it to come from every direction, to breathe into these dead bodies, and to bring them back to life."

By this time Ezekiel had a little more confidence. He spoke to the wind and, sure enough, breath entered the bodies and they came to life! There were enough of them to form an army, But Ezekiel wasn't afraid. They were friendly. Even if they hadn't been, Ezekiel was standing on the Lord's side, and that looked like a very good place to be.

God said to Ezekiel, "The people of Israel are like these bones. They say that they are dried up, without any hope and with no future. So tell them that I, the Sovereign Lord, am going to open their graves. . . . I will put my breath in them, bring them back to life, and let them live in their own land. Then they will know that I am the Lord."

Ezekiel breathed, too — a sigh of relief. He knew one thing for sure: If God, the sovereign Lord, said he would do something, he would do it!

What is this story *really* about?

The Spirit of God:

The spirit of God is working in us, blowing where it will and when it will. But we mustn't wait for it — sitting and doing nothing. Ezekiel was ready for the Spirit to work through him. We must be ready, too. What can we do to "get ready"?

Hope:

Ezekiel's first visit to the valley was to prophesy doom, but his second visit was to carry the message of hope. If any situation ever seemed hopeless, Israel's did; but Israel rose from its "grave" of exile. We should never abandon hope.

Let's *talk* about it!

THE HANDWRITING ON THE WALL
(Daniel 5)

There's an old saying folks use when something bad happens to someone for good reason: "He should have seen the handwriting on the wall." In other words, the signs were there, if he or she had only looked.

That saying is older than you might think. In fact, it refers to something that happened long before the birth of Christ:

There once was a king of Babylon named Belshazzar. He wasn't a man of good character. He liked drinking and partying more than he liked tending to business.

One night the king gave a huge party for a thousand people. While they were lounging in the banquet hall and getting drunk on wine, he rememberd that many gold and silver bowls and cups were stored in his palace. This was not ordinary dinnerware, even in kingly terms. These bowls and cups had been stolen from the Temple in Jerusalem. They were sacred vessels.

Wouldn't it be fun, Belshazzar thought, to use those holy bowls and cups for unholy purposes! So he sent his servants to fetch them. As soon as the fine vessels arrived, they were filled with wine, and the guests began drinking from them, raising them in toast to gods made of gold, silver, bronze, iron, wood, and stone. They laughed and drank and had a big time, until suddenly a very spooky thing happened.

A human hand appeared — just a hand, no body — and began writing on the wall of the palace! Well, cups and bowls stopped in mid-toast. Some even fell to the floor as the drunken guests shook with fright. The king's knees were rattling so badly he could hardly stand up. He did the only thing he knew to do — he screamed for his wizards, magicians, and astrologers. By the time they arrived, the hand had disappeared but the writing remained.

"What does this mean?" Belshazzar yelled. "Someone explain the handwriting on the wall! If you tell me what it means, I'll dress you in royal robes, put a gold chain of honor around your neck, and make you third in power in this kingdom."

That would be nice. Every one of the sorcerers would like that honor! It might even be worth lying for . . . but, no, they were frightened too, and who could guess what the consequences might be for lying about such a magical thing. They shook their heads.

King Belshazzar turned deathly pale. Even the red flush of wine disappeared from his skin. This worried the people, because he was their king, their leader! "Someone summon the queen mother! She will know what to do."

When Mother arrived, she fussed over him, as any worried mother would, and then she made a suggestion.

"There is a man in your kingdom," she said, "who has the spirit of the holy gods in him. . . . He has unusual ability and is wise and skillful in interpreting dreams, solving riddles, and explaining mysteries; so send for this man Daniel, and he will tell you what all this means."

When Daniel was brought in, Belshazzar offered him the same deal he offered the wizards — robes, gold chain, and power. Daniel didn't want it. He told the king to keep it or give it to someone else. He would, however, read the message and interpret it.

Daniel said to the king, "Remember King Nebuchadnezzar? He was a great king — majestic and dignified. But he became so taken with himself and with his power that he turned cruel and proud and stubborn. Because of this, God removed him from his throne, and sent him to live like a wild animal in the woods for seven years." To drive in the point, Daniel added, "His hair grew as long as eagle feathers and his nails as long as bird claws."

King Belshazzar grew even more pale.

"Even though you knew all this," Daniel continued, "you acted against the Lord of heaven and brought in the cups and bowls taken from his Temple. You, your noblemen, your wives, and your concubines drank wine out of them and praised gods made of gold, silver, bronze, iron, wood, and stone — gods that cannot see or hear and that do not know anything. But you did not honor the God who determines whether you live or die and who controls everything you do. That is why God has sent the hand to write these words."

King Belshazzar sat down.

The words on the wall were: *Mene, Mene, Tekel, Parsin.* Daniel said, "Number, number, weight, divisions. . . . God has numbered the days of your kingdom and brought it to an end; you have been weighed on the scales and found to be too light; your kingdom is divided up and given to the Medes and Persians."

King Belshazzar felt sick. He was finished and he knew it, but he could still do one good thing, one noble thing — he could honor his promise to Daniel, even if Daniel didn't want it. So he ordered his servants to dress Daniel in a robe of royal purple and to hang a gold chain of honor around his neck. Then he made him third in power in the kingdom.

That same night Balshazzar of Babylonia was killed, and Darius the Mede became king. The Hand had written it on the wall!

What is this story *really* about?

Awareness:

Our physical "senses' of sight, sound, smell, touch, and taste are important to us. We sharpen them daily. But we have other "senses," too — sense of confidence, sense of worth, sense of awareness. Can you name some more? For our own good, we should keep our sense of awareness sharp, able to perk up at the first sign of "handwriting on the wall." Have you ever seen "handwriting on the wall"? Were you able to do something about it, or was it too late? If we see it, we at least have a chance to erase it!

Blasphemy:

Blasphemy sounds like an old-fashioned word. Maybe it is. What does it mean to you (irreverence, sacrilege, profanity)? How do you feel when someone curses or uses abusive language in your presence? What do you do about it, if anything? How do you think a Christian should respond to "blasphemy"?

Honor:

King Belshazzar honored his promise to Daniel, even though he knew it would not help him. To be called an "honorable" person is to receive an extremely high compliment. What does being "honorable" mean to you? How does it relate to the Christian life?

Let's *talk* about it!

GOD NAMES THE CHILDREN

(Hosea 1:2-9;3)

The prophet Hosea was worried about the future of his country, Israel. The unfaithful people were worshiping idols instead of God. They were fickle, just like unfaithful wives and husbands. How could he turn them around? How could he make them understand the terrible consequences of their fickleness?

Since he was a very good preacher and had some success with illustrations, he decided to draw a parallel between an unfaithful wife and an unfaithful Israel. In his heart he was thinking of his own situation — of Gomer, his beautiful young wife, who wandered off from time to time. So he preached and preached about unfaithfulness . . . and nothing happened.

Meanwhile, Gomer began bearing children, and the Lord stepped in to help Hosea with his preaching.

"I will name your children," the Lord said, "and they will become symbols to remind the people continually of my disappointment, my anger, and my power."

Hosea thought that was a great idea. His own children would be walking sermon illustrations.

So God named the children.

The first was a son. "Call him Jezreel," the Lord said. Jezreel was a city. (Have you ever thought of naming a child after a city? Maybe Pittsburg Smith? Or Albuquerque Johnson?) Jezreel was where an Israelite king, Jehu, had fought an unusually cruel revolution in the Lord's name. The king's intentions may have been good, but he went too far, and God was angry about it.

"Your child, Jezreel," God said to Hosea, "will be a symbol of things gone wrong and a reminder that I will take revenge on the house of Jehu — yes, on Israel."

Hosea's second child was a daughter, and the name God chose for her was . . . Unloved. (Imagine going through life with a name like that!) The reason he named her "Unloved" was so that she could symbolize God's lack of mercy for his people, the Israelites. When those people looked at little "Unloved," they would be reminded that God's love and forgiveness were beyond reach.

Gomer bore Hosea one more child, a son, before she left home for the last time. God gave this child a hyphenated name — "Not-My-People." (Another good name for a newborn might be "Cries-Too-Much.") Hosea's son, Not-My-People, would signify the breaking of the bond between God and Israel. He would symbolize no hope for the future.

It seemed so final. Would Israel never be redeemed? Would the wandering wife never come back?

One day, several years later, Hosea was walking through the marketplace, squeezing fruit and inspecting trinkets, when he noticed a group of slaves for sale. One of them looked familiar. He moved closer to get a better look. It was a woman in dirty, tattered clothes. Her face was haggard and sad, her body shrunken. Still, he knew her. This pitiful creature was Gomer, his wife, no longer young, no longer beautiful. Hosea bought her for fifteen pieces of silver and seven bushels of barley. It took a long time of nurturing and repentance, but Gomer and Hosea were able to love each other once again.

This reconciliation made Hosea think very deeply: Perhaps Jezreel, Unloved, and Not-My-People were not final symbols after all. Maybe Gomer was God's best symbol all along, the perfect sermon illustration.

His thoughts led to prayer, and the prayer to prophecy: "The time will come," he said, "when the people of Israel will once again turn to the Lord their God and to a descendant of David their king. Then they will fear the Lord and will receive his good gifts."

What is this story *really* about?

Fickleness:

Have you ever had a friend, whom you thought was special, but who left you for someone else? Do you know people who flit like butterflies from cause to cause, supporting whatever is popular at the time? Do you know someone who changes churches frequently, always searching for something different? These people are fickle. Have you ever been a fickle person? What's wrong with it?

Reconciliation:

It has been said that the best part of an argument is the "making up." Do you agree? Differences can be turned into assets and used to strengthen our commitments to one another. How can that be?

Let's *talk* about it!

THE INVASION OF LOCUSTS
(Book of Joel)

Joel of the Old Testament was a prophet with one message, and that message was: Repent! He was an eloquent speaker, a poet who could touch the hearts of people and move them to action. So the Lord gave Joel a unique opportunity, a graphic illustration, and told him to make the most of it, which he did.

God sent a swarm of locusts to invade the land. Locusts are short-horned grasshoppers that fly and crawl in enormous, unstoppable armies, leaving destruction and devastation behind them.

Joel said of the locusts, "They have destroyed our grapevines and chewed up our fig trees. They have stripped off the bark, till the branches are white. . . . In front of them the land is like the Garden of Eden, but behind them is a barren desert. Nothing escapes them."

Those of us who have never experienced a "locust plague" first-hand can't begin to appreciate how terrible it is; yet this appreciation is necessary, if we're to understand Joel's concern. Let's look at some facts from our own history.

In the 1870s during the westward movement locusts swarmed, stopping covered wagons for days at a time while they ate every blade of grass, every piece of fruit, and every vegetable in sight, leaving nothing for the travelers or their animals. During that same decade, reports came out of Nebraska that the sky was darkened by a swarm that was one hundred miles wide and three hundred miles long! Just imagine that many bugs!

From 1930 to 1940, locusts caused considerble damage to our own Pacific coast, and during the summers of 1938, '39, and '40, they attacked our northern Great Plains.

Even more recently, in June 1991, American grasshoppers hatched in record numbers and in two weeks consumed nearly 50,000 acres of citrus leaves, hayfields, and pine forests along central Florida's west coast. This was the largest swarm in the southeastern United States since the 1950s.

Most interesting of all, though, is the locust attack on Jerusalem in 1915. It was documented by John D. Whiting in *The National Geographic Magazine* in December of that year. This is not a remote Bible story about people with strange customs and odd clothing. It is a story that our own grandparents and great-grandparents can relate to, for it happened in their time. One thing we know for sure from this Twentieth Century plague is that Joel's description is accurate.

According to observers, the first indication of locusts was the noise — a loud sound of flapping wings. Next came the blocking of the sun, as happened in Nebraska. And finally, when they were overhead, Mr. Whiting reports: "(there came) . . . a veritable shower of their excretions, which fell thick and fast and resembled those of mice." Yes, it was terrible. But there is more.

When they attacked trees, leaves would fall like rain, leaving nothing but bare bark, just as Joel had said. And, as in the American West, they destroyed food — fruit trees, vegetable plants, and melon fields. They also ate ants, bees, honey, and each other.

There were so many of them they turned white roads black. Horses slipped on them and lost their footing. Pedestrians could not avoid crushing them with every step. They entered homes by crawling up walls and squeezing through cracks. People constantly swept and killed . . . and plucked them out of clothing.

The locusts stayed in Jerusalem for several days, then left, literally, for "greener pastures," something new to destroy.

By the time they got to Bethlehem, the rains came and drove them to the ground, where they began dying. That still wasn't the end of it. The stench was nearly unbearable. And, what do you do with tons of dying locusts? Most were buried, some were dried and used as fuel, some were roasted and eaten — the natives said they tasted like fish.

A locust plague is a terrible thing. When it happened in Joel's time, he took it as a sign of God's displeasure and called the people to repent. Evidently, they responded to his message, because he followed with words of comfort and a promise that God would renew the land and fill the people with his Spirit.

Perhaps Joel's greatest contribution to all of us who have lived since, is his poetic passage about the outpouring of the Holy Spirit following the locust plague. It was so memorable that the apostle Paul quoted it on the Day of Pentecost:

> I will pour out my Spirit
> on everyone.
> Your sons and daughters will
> proclaim my message;
> your young men will see visions,
> and your old men will have dreams.

What is this story *really* about?

Repentance:

Remorse means simply "feeling sorry." Repentance means feeling sorry and then making a "change," either of mind or direction.

Let's say, for example, that a person drinks and drives and has an accident in which an innocent person is hurt. The drinker not only feels sorry, but makes a change — he or she quits drinking.

True repentance will bring this drinker many personal benefits. Name some. How does repentance relate to Christianity?

Let's *talk* about it!

The struggle between church and state is not new. It isn't even old. It is extremely old, going back hundreds of more years than we would care to count.

Consider Amos the Prophet, representing God or "the church," and Amaziah, an idolatrous priest whom you probably never heard of, representing the king or "the state." These two men had quite a confrontation somewhere around seven hundred and fifty years before Christ, and that wasn't even the first such clash of church and state.

Amos was a farmer who lived in a small town in Judah. He had a few sheep and some fig trees and plenty of time to meditate, pray, and think about God's laws and God's people. He saw that the rich were getting richer, the poor poorer, and not many were left in the middle. Add to that the Baal worship learned from the Canaanites, and the corruption seeping into the guilds of professional prophets, and it was easy for him to see that the entire land was in need of social reform.

While Amos was pondering the problem, God spoke to him, calling him to be a prophet, giving him the opportunity to make changes. Amos was different, because he wasn't a professional prophet. He didn't belong to the guilds, where members were trained to go into trances, and he didn't accept pay for his prophecies, as many prophets were now doing. He was a "free spirit," calling it as he saw it, delivering God's message of what would happen if things didn't change. What would happen, of course, was not pretty, and that was how Amos came to be called the "Prophet of Doom." He made folks uncomfortable.

Amaziah, chief priest of the Baal religion at Bethel, where God had sent Amos, noticed the unrest among the people. It made him nervous. It made him worry about his position as one of the officials of the kingdom. Was he secure?

What could he do about this Amos person? . . . After much thought Amaziah decided to report Amos to the king and gain some royal favor, a little insurance for himself, at the same time.

So he sent a letter, accusing Amos of treason. He based his charge on what he claimed were Amos's words — that the king would die in battle and that the people of Israel would be taken away from their land. In those days prophets were commonly involved in revolutionary activities, so Amaziah knew the king would pay attention and would consider Amos a dangerous man.

As soon as he had sent the letter, Amaziah confronted Amos personally.

"That's enough, prophet!" he cried. "Go on back to Judah and do your preaching there. Let them pay you for it. Don't prophesy here at Bethel anymore. This is the king's place of worship, the national temple." Amaziah made it very clear that he had the authority of the king behind him.

Amos replied in his usual forthright manner, making it equally clear that he had the authority of God behind him!

"I am not the kind of prophet who prophesies for pay," he said. "I am a herdsman, and I take care of fig trees. But the Lord took me from my work as a shepherd and ordered me to come and prophesy to his people Israel. So now listen to what the Lord says."

Amos then prophesied in personal terms, so that Amaziah could not possibly misunderstand.

"Amaziah, the Lord says to you, 'Your wife will become a prostitute in the city, and your children will be killed in war. Your land will be divided up and given to others, and you yourself will die in a heathen country.'"

The kinds of things that Amos described were not unusual at that time. Those who were victorious in battle commonly raped women, killed children, confiscated land, and drove leaders away. So Amaziah knew exactly what Amos was talking about. That, however was just the small picture. The large one, which Amos also drew, was of the rape, murder, pillage, and exile of an entire nation.

Who won? Church or state? . . . The Bible story ends without an answer. We do know that Amos' prophecy concerning the fate of Israel was fulfilled. We also know that it didn't end there. Nor did it end in the next century or the next. The struggle between church and state didn't end either. It goes on to this day. Maybe it's healthy. Maybe it keeps us spiritually alert. It certainly keeps us on our toes!

What is this story *really* about?

Conflict:

Each of us deals with conflict daily, even if it's no more than a calendar conflict, and each conflict must be resolved, if we're to have peace of mind. How do you deal with conflict? Are you a procrastinator? Or do you strike immediately?

This story points up the conflict between church and state. Do you see any evidence of such conflict in your own church or in your own city? How would you resolve the ongoing conflict concerning prayer in schools? One city had a problem with placing a nativity scene in front of the courthouse at Christmas time. How would you resolve that?

Let's *talk* about it!

THE RELUCTANT MISSIONARY
(Book of Jonah)

Jonah did not want to go to Nineveh, even though God Himself had commanded it. He objected to the reason for going.

"Go preach," God had said.

That was okay. Jonah was a prophet. He could preach.

"Go preach in Nineveh," God had said.

That was okay, too. Nineveh was a city full of sinners. They needed preaching.

"Tell the people of Nineveh that I will destroy their city in forty days," God had said.

That was the problem. Jonah knew God very well. He knew that God would not destroy those sinners if they repented. Such a kind and forgiving God! Usually, Jonah liked it that way, but not this time. Those heartless, cruel people of Nineveh were Israel's worst enemies. They deserved destruction! If they were forgiven, God would have made a terrible mistake.

Jonah didn't want any part of that, so he ran away to a ship bound for Tarshish, paid his fare, and went to sleep. (Think this is going to be another big fish story? Wrong! The fish is a minor character.)

Jonah, once he was comfortable on the ship, thought he had escaped God. Ha! Can anyone escape God? Well, God dumped him in the water — man overboard! — and he was swallowed by, yes, that big fish that finally spit him out on dry land. Exasperated, Jonah sat on the beach and raised his hand to God.

"Okay, okay, God. You've made your point. I'll go to Nineveh," he said. "But, mind you, I don't go willingly. I go because you're forcing me!"

So Jonah went to Nineveh and gave those sinners the message — a hot and heavy one, just like the weather.

Everyone was sweating! He preached like he never preached before, putting the fear of God into them so properly that they all repented, every last one of them, including their king. Yes, the king himself came down from his throne, exchanged his robes for sackcloth, and sat in ashes!

Nineveh's humiliation before God was complete. And, just as Jonah had predicted . . . God forgave them.

"See, didn't I tell you!"

"Forgiveness is God's nature, Jonah. He didn't change his nature. He just changed his mind. Didn't you ever change your mind?"

"Hmmph."

What did Jonah do? . . . He sulked. Oh, he was a great sulker. For days he sat in the blistering hot sun, sulking, just because God did not do as Jonah thought he ought. Jonah hung his head . . . squinted his eyes . . . pushed out his lower lip . . . and got a sunburn he'd never forget! He had wanted so much to see those wicked people punished. He truly believed that God had made a mistake.

Well, it got hotter out there, and still he sat. He was so pitiful that God — the kind and loving God — in his compassion, put a plant behind him for shade. A castor oil plant, by the way. But the next day God "changed his mind" and commanded a worm to eat it up. That made Jonah mad! He jumped up and down like a little troll, while the hot sun beat at his head and the scorching wind whipped at his face. God had let him down, taking even that bit of shade, that poor little bush, away!

"I would rather be dead!" he screamed.

And God said, quietly, "Jonah, are you angry because the plant died?"

"Yes, Lord! I have a right to be angry!"

"This plant grew up in one night and disappeared the next," God said. "You didn't do anything for it and you didn't make it grow — yet you feel sorry for it! How much more, then, should I have pity on Nineveh. After all, it has more than

120,000 innocent children in it." . . . You can bet Jonah gave that some serious thought!

Did he repent? Did he admit he was wrong? . . . We will never know by reading the Bible, because it doesn't tell us. It is enough to understand what God tells us: All the world is a mission field, even the "Ninevehs," and all who believe in God have a mission to fulfill.

You see — there's a lot more to Jonah than just a big fish story!

What is this story *really* about?

Hiding from God:

Jonah tried to hide from God. Have you ever wished you could hide from God? Why? Sometimes we ignore things, hoping they'll go away. Can we get rid of God by ignoring him? What happens if we try?

Forgiveness:

If God could forgive the people of Nineveh — the cruelest, meanest, most hateful people you can possibly imagine — we should be able to forgive anyone who harms us. It's hard, but God sets the example.

Mission Work:

The "mission field" isn't necessarily thousands of miles away. Nineveh might be in our own backyard. Did you know that missionaries come to the United States from other countries? It's true. How can we be missionaries in our own country? In our own church? In our own families? Why is this more difficult than going away to be missionaries?

Let's *talk* about it!

(The story of Jonah is adapted from *"Five Men Touched by God"* by Janet Litherland. Copyright © 1978, Meriwether Publishing Ltd.)

ENOUGH IS ENOUGH, NINEVEH!
(Book of Nahum)

"The Lord God tolerates no rivals;
   he punishes those who oppose him.
   In his anger he pays them back.
The Lord does not easily become angry,
   but he is powerful
   and never lets the guilty go unpunished."

That is what the prophet Nahum said to get everyone's attention. . . . It got mine! . . . Did it get yours?

God "never lets the guilty go unpunished." That's a little different view of our loving, compassionate, forgiving, merciful God, isn't it?

Think of yourself as a loving, compassionate, forgiving, merciful Christian. And imagine an enemy — someone who hates you and everything you stand for. Someone who tells lies about you, who is treacherous and deceitful, who makes fun of your Christianity, who charms away your friends, who hurts the ones you love, who stomps on your toes and spits in your face. . . . If you're normal, there will come a time when you'll shout, "Enough is enough!" And you'll flatten that enemy with a swift, hard, punch in the nose!

That's exactly what God did to Nineveh. He flattened that city and all of its rotten-to-the-core citizens. What could they possibly have done to make our merciful God that angry? With God, just how much is "enough"? . . . Let's find out.

Nineveh was the capital of the Assyrian empire, an arrogant, cruel, and oppressive nation. Its citizens terrorized all countries in what was then thought to be the whole world. They would conquer cities and deport entire populations, as they did in Judah when they took more than two hundred thousand people into slavery. They attacked nearby Babylon, carried off its precious (to them) statues of gods and burned the city. Everywhere they went they vandalized, looted, and murdered. . . . Was that enough for God?

These Assyrian terrorists went all the way to Egypt and captured its capital city, Thebes, where Nahum says they beat children in the streets and took their parents into exile. . . . Was that enough?

These barbarians proudly recorded their atrocities on walls, which were excavated just a little over a hundred years ago — their own drawings show captives staked to the ground, being skinned alive! . . . Enough is enough, Nineveh!

The prophet Nahum closed his eyes and relayed God's message:

"Nineveh, you are under attack!
The power that will shatter you has come.
    Prepare for battle!
The Lord is about to restore the glory of Israel
    as it was before her enemies plundered her."

Then Nahum drew a picture with God's words, a picture of what would happen to Nineveh:

"Chariots dash wildly through the streets,
    rushing back and forth in the city squares.
The gates by the river burst open;
    the palace is filled with terror.
The queen is taken captive.
Like water from a broken dam
    the people rush from Nineveh!
'Stop! Stop!' the cry rings out —
    but no one turns back.

Nineveh is destroyed, deserted, desolate!
    Hearts melt with fear;
    knees tremble, strength is gone;
    faces grow pale.
Where now is the city
    that was like a den of lions?

Doomed is the lying, murderous city,
    full of wealth to be looted and plundered!
Listen! The crack of the whip,
    the rattle of wheels.

Horsemen charge, swords flash, spears gleam!
Corpses are piled high,
    dead bodies without number.
Nineveh the whore is being punished.
Attractive and full of deadly charms,
    she enchanted nations and enslaved them.
The Lord Almighty says,
'I will punish you, Nineveh!
I will strip you naked
and let the nations see you,
see you in all your shame.'"

Nahum's prophecy came true. Nineveh fell at the hands of her old (and very capable!) enemy, Babylon, who "did unto Nineveh" as Nineveh had done unto everyone else.

News of the fall spread quickly. People everywhere rose to their feet, wiped the dust from their clothes and the tears from their eyes, and began clapping their hands . . . clapping, clapping, and clapping . . . until the entire world echoed with the sounds of their joy and relief!

That was enough.

What is this story *really* about?

Sin:

Sin, in the Old Testament, is the people's failure to keep the covenant God made with them; that is, that he would be their God and they would be his people. Basically, that's still what sin is — a break with God through wrongdoing. How do you feel about the sins of Nineveh? Are comparable sins being committed in our cities today? What are they? What is being done about them? What are God's people doing about them?

Justice:

God's justice in Old Testament times seems exceedingly harsh, particularly what he did to Nineveh. But Nineveh's sins were harsh, too. How do you feel about "eye for an eye" justice?

When Nineveh was finally destroyed, people everywhere rejoiced. Were they gloating? Were they showing loyalty to

God? Was it right for them to rejoice? Is it ever right to rejoice at another's misfortune?

Corruption:

Do you suppose Nineveh was always wicked? How do you suppose the corruption of this city happened? Do you think one person could possibly have corrupted the whole city? The writer of Hebrews cautions us with these words: "Let no one become like a bitter plant that grows up and causes many troubles with its poison." (Hebrews 12:15)

Let's *talk* about it!

LET'S GET THIS TEMPLE REBUILT!
(Book of Haggai)

When the Jews returned to Jerusalem from captivity, everything was in ruins — broken walls, overgrown floors, abandoned personal items. What a disheartening sight! Still, it was theirs. They were home, and they could rebuild their houses. The Temple, however, was another matter. It had been burned. The beautiful bronze columns had been broken in pieces and carted away by Nebuchadnezzar's army. Also gone were workers' tools, the bowls and utensils used in services of worship, and everything made of gold or silver. All that was left were the courts and the altar, and that had been irreverently toppled.

The people re-set the altar immediately and began having daily worship, but they didn't think about rebuilding the Temple right away. The project was so enormous it overwhelmed them. "The time isn't right," they said, excusing themselves.

Most of the people who returned were poor, which had a lot to do with it, but as years passed, they grew accustomed to the way things were, and the idea of rebuilding the Temple just wasn't brought up.

Then one day along came Haggai, an energetic and enthusiastic prophet who looked around and said, "Let's get this Temple rebuilt!" He made the people take a look, too — a good, long look at themselves.

"You are all living in nice houses, sturdy houses," he cried, "but the Lord has no Temple. Aren't you ashamed?" The people shrugged, turning their pockets inside out.

"You say you have no means. Have you stopped to consider why? . . . You plant a lot but harvest little. You have food and wine, but not enough to make you full; you have clothing, but not enough to keep you warm; and workers cannot earn a decent wage! Can't you see? The Lord has blown away your harvest. He is unhappy because his Temple lies in ruins while every one of you works on his own house!"

Haggai's words were extremely effective — work on the Temple began within three weeks! Even the governor, Zerubbabel, and Joshua, the high priest, got involved, and they proved to be excellent, dedicated leaders for the project.

As sometimes happens, though, people's enthusiasm began to fade. The old folks, those who could remember the original Temple, were especially discouraged and discouraging. "Even if we rebuild it," they said, "we will never be able to replace the treasures that Nebuchadnezzar carried away. It will never be as splendid as it once was."

So Haggai turned to the Lord for help. The Lord decided to speak through his prophet: "Don't be discouraged, any of you," he said to his people. "Do the work, for I am with you. . . . Before long I will shake heaven and earth, land and sea. I will overthrow all the nations, and their treasures will be brought here, and the Temple will be filled with wealth. The new Temple will be more splendid than the old one, and there I will give my people prosperity and peace."

It's amazing what God can do. Especially when he speaks out loud. These pitiful people returned to work with more energy than ever before. Even so, Haggai continued to encourage them. "Remember," he said, "holiness is not contagious, but sin is. You must work at holiness, and God will reward you."

Five years later, with the help of Zechariah, another inspired prophet, God rewarded them. The work was completed.

Sometimes it just takes a little push.

What is this story *really* about?

Thoughtlessness:

The people of Jerusalem weren't against the rebuilding of the Temple; they just didn't think about it. This upset God.

We often hurt people without intending to; we just don't think. Can you give examples of thoughtlessness? What might the consequences be? How can we help ourselves (and one another) to be more thoughtful?

Discouragement:

Have you ever been so overwhelmed that you just gave up? Too many bills to pay, too many dishes to wash, too many weeds to pull, too much company to entertain, too much work to get done? What's the use? . . . What is the use?

God says to us, "Don't be discouraged, any of you. Do the work, for I am with you." (2:4) Does that really help? After all, God doesn't pick up a shovel.

Let's *talk* about it!

A vision is an imaginative way of looking into the future. In a religious sense it is God's revelation in "picture" form. With the possible exception of Balaam the Diviner, these visions were given only to holy men who were serving God.

Zechariah was a holy man who was serving God very well, so well that God gave him eight visions in a single night! These visions were like dreams, meant to encourage the Israelites to finish the rebuilding of the Temple, started under Haggai's ministry. This was important to God.

Haggai had emphasized the material prosperity that the Temple would bring to Judah, which got the people started; but Zechariah focused on spiritual glories, and that was what kept folks going when they bogged down under hard work and strained nerves. Let's use our imaginations to leaf through a Bible-times scrapbook. We'll take a look at the pictures that did such a good job of inspiring the people of Zechariah's time. Maybe they'll inspire us. We, too, get bogged down with hard work and stress.

1. The first picture shows God's special love for the Israelites.

An angel is riding a red horse through a beautiful valley. He stops among some myrtle trees where there are other horses — red, dappled, and white. Zechariah asks the angel,

"What do the horses mean?"

The angel says that the horses have just returned from a trip around the world. They were inspecting it for the Lord.

"And what did they find?" Zechariah asks.

The angel replies, "They found that the whole world is helpless and without hope."

Then the angel turns his attention to God and asks, "How much longer will you be angry with the people of Judah? It's been seventy years now."

The Lord answers, "I love my people and am concerned for them. Other nations are making them suffer more than is necessary. I will help the people restore my Temple and rebuild my holy city. I am coming back to Jerusalem."

2. The second picture shows that God's enemies have been destroyed and that no one will oppose the rebuilding.

There is an angel with four ox horns. Zechariah asks the angel, "What do these horns mean?"

The angel replies, "They are the world powers that scattered the Israelites." Then the angel points to four workmen with hammers and says, "These men have come to pound their hammers on the horns, to crush the nations that crushed Judah."

3. The third picture shows Jerusalem outgrowing its walls.

A man with a measuring stick is hurrying through the city. Zechariah asks, "Where are you going?"

"To measure Jerusalem," he answers. "I'm not sure there's enough room for all the people!"

Then two angels appear. One says to the other, "Run and tell that young man that Jerusalem will be too big for walls. There's no need for them anyway. God himself will become the wall."

4. The fourth picture shows that the Messiah is on the way.

Joshua is standing before the Lord. His clothes are very dirty. Satan stands there too, ready to accuse Joshua of many things, but the Lord stops him. God orders his angels to put clean clothes and a new turban on Joshua. He says, "I have taken away your sins and given you new clothes to wear."

Then the Lord puts Joshua in charge of the Temple as High Priest. He says, "I will reveal my servant, who is called The Branch . . . and in a single day I will take away the sin of this land."

5. The fifth picture shows God's people receiving his grace and blessings through their spiritual leaders.

Zechariah sees a seven-branched candelabrum made of gold. There is one olive tree on each side of the candelabrum. He asks the angel, "What do these things stand for?"

The angel answers, "The seven candles are the seven eyes of the Lord. They see all over the earth."

"What do the trees mean?"

"These are the two men whom God has chosen and anointed to serve him."

6. The sixth picture shows the effect that the rebuilt Temple and the teaching of God's law will have on wickedness.

Zechariah can't believe his eyes! A giant book is flying through the air! It is thirty feet long and fifteen feet wide! He is so amazed he can't speak.

The angel answers his unasked question. "The book says that every thief and liar will be taken away and their homes left in ruins."

7. The seventh picture shows God forgiving and removing sin.

No sooner has the flying book gone by than another object comes sailing through the air. It is a bushel basket with a lid on it. As Zechariah watches, the lid pops up, revealing a woman inside!

The angel explains, "She represents the sins of the world." Then the angel pushes her down and snaps the lid back on.

Two other women with powerful wings come swooping down. They snatch up the basket and fly off with it.

"Where are they taking it?" asks Zechariah.

"To Babylonia," the angel replies. "The people there will place it in a temple and worship it."

8. The last picture shows God's protective power.

Four chariots, drawn by different colored horses, are coming from between two bronze mountains. As Zechariah watches, they go off in different directions.

"What does this mean?" he asks.

"They have just come from the presence of the Lord," the angel answers. "They are on their way to inspect the earth."

What is this story *really* about?

Inspiration:

Zechariah inspired the people of his time. Who inspires people these days (in our nation, our cities, our churches, our families)? How do they do it? What inspires you?

Encouragement:

Have you ever struggled all alone at something with no encouragement from anyone? It's hard to tackle big jobs without encouragement. Family members are usually encouraging; friends sometimes are. Why do many people find it difficult to encourage others?

What Goes Around Comes Around:

Did you notice that in Zechariah's first vision the horses had just returned from an inspection of the world, and that in his eighth vision they were leaving for another inspection of the world? What happened in between? Did they expect to find a change on the second trip? What do you think?

Let's *talk* about it!

PART III:
THE NEW TESTAMENT STORIES

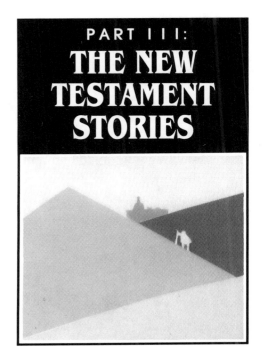

EIGHT BLESSINGS AND EIGHT CURSES
(Matthew 5:3-10;21:23-28;23:1-33)

There's a popular song about Santa Claus that says, "He's makin' a list, checkin' it twice, gonna find out who's naughty and nice."* All of us make lists. We make lists of things we have to do, of items we need at the store, or of people we want to talk with. We make "wish lists" of things we'd like to have someday. You know — a new house, a sailboat, a million dollars! We also make practical "wish lists" of things we'd like to accomplish in, say, six months — like a diet. Or in six years — perhaps an education. There are even some people who make lists of what they intend to achieve in a lifetime! It's the order of things that attracts us to lists. Lists are "neat" in both senses of the word!

There are many lists in the Bible. Moses, for example, gave us a list of Ten Commandments. Paul listed the Fruits of the Spirit for us. But two very interesting lists are given to us by Jesus Himself: A list of Eight Blessings (The Beatitudes) and a list of Eight Curses (The Woes).

Picture this: Jesus is walking along the shore of a beautiful lake — the Jews call this lake the Sea of Galilee, though it really is a fishing lake with green foliage and hot springs. A beautiful place! And because it is such a beautiful and desirable place, many other people have gathered there, too — so many people that the crowds begin to make Jesus uncomfortable. What he really wants, and needs, is a quiet place in which to meditate and talk privately with a few of his followers.

Very slowly he moves away from the crowd and into the hills, with some of his friends trailing behind. The air is clean and fresh, the ground is soft, and the chatter of the people soon begins to fade.

After a time, Jesus finds the spot he's looking for — a grassy hill with lots of room all around. He climbs to the top and sits down. It's quiet. . . . He prays, first silently and then aloud, and then he begins thinking aloud. His followers, who by now have seated themselves comfortably around him, perk up their ears. They are used to his profound sayings, but these words seem more, uh . . . direct. . . . Yes! Jesus is teaching. They sit up straight and focus their attention. It is time to learn, to gather even more wisdom from this gifted teacher.

. . . But what is this? A list? As they listen, they realize that each item on the list states two things — what God expects from them, and what they can expect from God. My! This is interesting!

"Let's see now," one whispers. "If I am humble or gentle of spirit, I will inherit the earth. Inherit the earth? Can this be true?"

In a few moments his friend whispers back, "If we are merciful to others, as God expects us to be, then we can expect God to be merciful to us!"

Jesus goes through five items on his list before the group notices that he is speaking much louder, more like preaching than teaching. Why is he doing this? It makes his listeners uneasy. They begin to squirm. Then someone looks around and . . . surprise — the crowd has followed them from the lake! (So interested were the "loyal few" in Jesus' list, they hadn't noticed. And, to be honest, the people had crept up quietly.) They aren't noisy now. They are seated quietly on the ground, listening attentively to the blessings, and Jesus has raised his voice to accommodate them. These blessings are clearly meant for everyone. Anyone.

At last Jesus says, "Blessed are you who are persecuted for doing God's work, for the kingdom of heaven is yours."

"What? Does he mean it?"

"Of course he does. Jesus doesn't say anything he doesn't mean."

"Well, now," says one of the men, rising to his feet, "I feel greatly encouraged."

This list of blessings was the beginning of Jesus' "Sermon on the Mount," or, "Sermon on the Hill," you might say, a sermon that has left its mark across the centuries and around the world.

Now take your mental eraser and erase that quiet picture of the gentle, kindly Jesus. . . . All erased? Then picture this: Jesus is in the Temple in Jerusalem. He is teaching by means of stories or "parables," and many people have gathered to hear him.

Enter the scribes, or lawyers, as we know them today. They are an official group trained in the law of Moses to interpret, teach, and judge.

Enter, too, the Pharisees. They are an unofficial group representing a school of thought that rigidly dictates right and wrong. Fanatical sort of folks.

"By what authority do you teach in this temple?" demands one of the lawyers.

Jesus answers, "I will ask you just one question, and if you give me an answer, I will tell you what right I have to do these things. Where did John's right to baptize come from? Was it from God or from man?"

They argue for a while among themselves, then finally answer, "We don't know."

"Neither will I tell you, then, by what right I do these things."

Well, they banter back and forth, the Pharisees even trying to catch Jesus in a mental trap, when finally the Lord's temper flares and he cries, "You hypocrites! You do not practice what you preach!" . . . Out comes his list — eight things that really bother him. Each item, as with the blessings, is two-fold. He states what these people say, then what they actually do.

"Woe unto you!" he cries. "You lock the door to the kingdom of heaven in people's faces, but you yourselves don't go in, nor do you allow in those who are trying to enter!" His voice isn't just loud — it's deafening — and all the more remarkable, coming from Jesus who is known to be gentle.

"You hypocrites!" he cries again. "You give to God one tenth, but you neglect to obey the really important teachings of the Law, such as justice and mercy and honesty. *You strain a fly out of your drink but swallow a camel!"*

On he goes, down through his list — five, six, seven, eight — crying "Woe!" and "Hypocrites!" and, finally, "Snakes and Sons of Snakes!" He is really upset with these people. At last, he declares the lawyers and Pharisees unsalvageable. Can you imagine? He condemns them to hell. . . . This is really scary to the rest of his audience, because they know that he's the One who actually holds the keys to heaven and hell. He does, indeed, have the authority questioned earlier.

Now erase that picture. (Gesture)

And this we read in Acts 3:26, "God chose his Servant and sent him to you, to bless you . . . and to make every one of you turn from your wicked ways."

Jesus makes lists. He checks them twice. He wants to find out who's naughty. And who's nice!

What is this story *really* about?

Orderliness:

Jesus conducted his business in an orderly manner. His entire life followed a pattern. Do you sometimes feel as if your life is out of control? What can we do to put order in our lives?

Encouragement:

Everyone needs encouragement. Jesus gives encouragement in the Beatitudes. Read Matthew 5:3-10. Do you know someone who needs encouragement? How can you help?

Hypocrisy:

Jesus got tough with hypocrites. What is a hypocrite? Read Matthew 23:1-33. What is wrong with being a hypocrite?

Anger:

Anger can be healthy — it's what we do with it that often gets us in trouble.

Let's *talk* about it!

---

*"Santa Claus is Comin' to Town" by Haven Gillespie and J. Fred Coots. Copyright © Leo Feist, Inc. 1934, 1962.

This is a "once upon a time" story. It could be last year or this year or any year. Once upon a time there was a twelve-year-old girl who was very, very sick; so sick, in fact, that she was dying, and nothing could be done to save her.

Her father, who was a lay-leader at their church, was beside himself with grief. He tried everything a father could do — doctors, medicines, even prayer — but nothing helped. Then he remembered hearing about the miracles performed by Jesus of Nazareth. And Jesus was in the area!

"Might it be possible," he asked himself, "that this person, Jesus, could heal my little girl? Oh, I love her so much!"

So Jairus (that was the father's name) went to the shore of the Sea of Galilee where a large crowd had gathered to hear Jesus speak. At first Jairus hesitated. To seek the help of an itinerant preacher was to go against the tradition of his church. What would people think?

Then in his mind he saw his little girl, lying helpless in her bed. Without giving it another thought, he stepped forward. As he spoke, he knelt at Jesus' feet. "Please!" he cried. "My little daughter is very sick. Please come and place your hands on her so that she will get well and live!" Jairus was humble and respectful. He was also very serious. He believed in the power of Jesus.

Jesus turned to him and said, "I'm sorry, but you can see that I'm very busy. I'm on a difficult schedule — after speaking to this group I must meet with city officials, then lunch at the Chamber of Commerce, after which I've a plane to catch."

. . . No! Jesus didn't say that! (That's what we might be tempted to say.) Jesus didn't say anything. He simply indicated to Jairus that he would follow him to his house, and they started off. The crowd followed.

Now it happened that along the way there was a problem, something that took extra time and delayed their trip. But it was important. A woman needed help and Jesus stopped to help her. During the delay, some people came running from Jairus' house with a terrible message.

"Your daughter has died," one of them said sadly. He put his arm around Jairus' shoulder. "Why bother this man any further?" They believed that while there was life there was hope, but . . . hope in death? Hardly.

Jesus paid no attention to this. He turned to Jairus and said, "Don't be afraid. Only believe."

Jairus was afraid all right, but he did believe. And so they went on. This time, though, Jesus didn't let the crowd follow. Only Peter, James, and John were allowed to go with them.

When they arrived at Jairus' house, there was noise and confusion. There were a lot of mourners and they were crying loudly. Some of them didn't even know the little girl — they were professional mourners. It was the custom in those days, you see, for even the poorest families in Israel to hire flute players and at least one person to wail at their funerals.

"Why do you make all this noise?" Jesus cried. Things got quiet in a hurry. "This child is not dead," he said. "She is only sleeping."

Well, the mourners knew better than that! Couldn't he see for himself? The man was crazy! And they started making fun of him.

Jesus sent them all ouside and shut the door. Only the child's father and mother and the three disciples would witness what happened next.

He took the child's hand and said, "Little girl, I tell you to get up." He not only said the words, he put the power of God into them. The little girl did as Jesus said. She got up at once and walked around the room. Those who saw it were amazed!

"Give her something to eat," Jesus said. And they did. Not only would she live, she was hungry, as hungry as any healthy twelve-year-old!

And how does this "once upon a time" story end? Why, "they lived happily ever after," of course!

Oh, there's one more thing. Jesus said, "Don't tell anyone about this miracle."

Shhhhhhhhhhhhhhhh!

Sometimes we need a little mystery in our lives, especially when it comes to the power of God.

What is this story *really* about?

Peer Pressure:

Jairus worried about asking Jesus for help because of what people would think. Jesus, after all, was just an itinerant preacher. Do you sometimes worry about what people will think if you do, or if you don't do, something? Why is that important? Can we change that kind of attitude? How?

Faith:

Once Jairus decided to approach Jesus, he did it with true faith. He really believed that Jesus could perform a miracle. Why is faith important to Christianity? Do miracles still happen today? Do you know of one you can share?

Timeliness:

Jesus didn't say to Jairus, "I'll be over next week." He went immediately. Sometimes we put off doing things. Is a belated effort better than none at all?

Let's *talk* about it!

Many of us have traveled at high noon in the middle of summer in the Deep South. And we have discovered that it's hot! Those of us who don't do well in the stifling heat have learned that it's much better to move through that territory in the cool of evening or even in the dark of night. But there's a problem with that. Unless we stick to the Interstate highways, where the exits have all-night service stations and restaurants, we're not likely to find gasoline, or a hamburger, or anyone to fix a leaky radiator.

Now just suppose you're on your way to Damascus — Damascus, Georgia, that is, down old Route 45 in the middle of the night. Your friend in the back seat is real hungry, but there aren't any restaurants open. There aren't any restaurants period. But there's a nice little house by the side of the road, and a light is shining from a back window. Someone is awake! You look at the mailbox and lo and behold — the name is Martin, your mother's maiden name. Surely these folks, these kinfolks, wouldn't mind fixing your friend a sandwich.

You pull into the driveway, step up on to the wooden porch, and knock on the door. You hear feet shuffling across the room, then a deep voice calls through the door, "Who's there?"

"Ummm . . . I'm a Martin. . . . From Pennsylvania?"

"You're a long way from home," the voice drawls, ominously.

"I wonder if you could, uh, give me a sandwich. Oh, not for me — it's for my friend. He's real hungry."

"Are you crazy? Can't you see I'm locked up for the night? My family's asleep. . . . A sandwich!" The feet shuffle away.

"Wait!" you call, knocking again. "This is real important."

"Go awaaaaay!"

You knock louder and cry out, "But you don't understand, sir. We're on our way to Damascus and there aren't any restaurants! My friend really is hungry. His stomach hurts."

Shuffle, shuffle, shuffle. The voice again sounds through the door. "A sandwich? That's all? Then you'll go away?"

"Yes, please. . . . I'm a Martin," you remind him, hopefully.

"Martins lived here before we moved in. Don't like Martins."

"Oh, well, really it's just my mother's maiden name. Pretty far removed, actually."

"Wait."

You pause in amazement. Wait? . . . And so you wait. You sit down in the old Brumby rocker and go back and forth, back and forth, back and forth . . .

In a few minutes the front door opens. There stands a craggy old man in a plaid bathrobe. In his extended hand is an impressive-looking sandwich. In his other hand is an impressive-looking shotgun!

You thank him profusely as you snatch the sandwich and back down the steps, smiling and bowing as you go, never taking your eyes off the gun.

This is one of the stories Jesus told his disciples. Well, sort of. He was teaching them to be persistent in prayer. He finished by saying, "Ask and you will receive; seek, and you will find; knock, and the door will be opened to you."

God welcomes our persistence, not because he can't hear or is too busy, or isn't persuaded, but because it is good for us. It helps us overcome pride, and selfishness, and indifference. He may not always give us what we want, but he will certainly give us what we need.

"Lord, help me find a parking place," a lady wailed one day. She desperately needed to get to the bank before it closed. "Please, Lord, just a parking place, that's all I ask."

Just then a car backed out ahead of her.

"Never mind, Lord," she said, quickly. "I found one."

What is this story *really* about?

Persistence:

God wants us to be persistent in prayer. Why? Why doesn't he answer our prayers immediately? How long should we keep trying to get an answer?

Wants and Needs:

How do wants and needs differ? Is it okay to pray for wants? God answers prayer in different ways. Think of some examples of God's answers in your own prayer life or that of your church.

Asking:

God takes care of us even when we don't ask him. However, if we ask him, in good faith, he will take even better care of us, just as we care for those we love. Read Luke 11:1-13.

Let's *talk* about it!

JESUS AT THE FESTIVAL OF SHELTERS
(John 7)

Festivals have always been a part of life, from earliest days right to the present. Everyone loves to celebrate! We have birthday parties, Fourth of July picnics, autumn revivals, Thanksgiving parades, Christmas candlelight services, New Year's Eve countdowns, and many other festive occasions during the year.

The people in Bible times also loved to celebrate, and one particularly happy time was the Festival of Shelters, held each year at the beginning of autumn. This eight-day festival celebrated the harvest and the prosperity everyone hoped for in the coming year.

Imagine a carnival-like atmosphere in downtown Jerusalem — things to see, things to do, and people everywhere! Families actually moved into the city, not to stay in hotels and motels, but in tiny shelters or tents (sometimes called "booths"), which they built themselves by weaving together branches and vines. In the center of the city was the largest shelter. It was called the "tent of meeting," where groups could gather. (This is where our expression "tent meeting," related to revival services, came from.)

In addition to meeting and eating, the Festival of Shelters was a religious festival. The shelters were meant to remind people of the way their ancestors lived while wandering in the wilderness and of their dependence on God. There were many sacrifices and many ceremonies. Each day the people would parade, waving branches and singing psalms, and each night they would chant the Psalms of Ascent from inside their shelters. It was a time of rejoicing and praising God.

Now at the particular festival in our story, the hottest topic of conversation was Jesus of Nazareth. Everyone was looking for him. He was a celebrity. However, the conversations were in whispers, because the Jewish authorities had forbidden people to discuss him and, in fact, had issued warrants for his arrest. He was just too controversial. Everyone seemed to have an opinion about this Jesus of Nazareth.

"He's a good man. Has character," one said.

"Maybe so, but he claims to be the Messiah. Isn't that blasphemous?"

"Oh, I don't know. He certainly has performed miracles — all that helping and healing."

"But the Messiah is descended from a royal line. He should come with mystery and splendor. We know this man. He comes from Galilee!"

(That's like saying, "He comes from Chicago. Can any good thing come from Chicago?") Why is it that we never take seriously someone in our own town who aspires to, even achieves, greatness. We always expect real heroes to come from somewhere else!

Well, besides those who liked Jesus and those who were undecided, there were those who were downright against him.

"As far as I'm concerned," someone said, "he's disturbing the peace and ought to be taken into custody."

"That's right! Whoever he is, he's definitely leading people astray!"

The air was certainly alive with excitement. But where was Jesus?

Truth is, he was already there. He had come quietly to the festival — no fanfare, no spectacle, just one of the crowd. Folks didn't even notice him until he suddenly started to preach openly. And what a marvelous idea that was! There at the Festival of Shelters, amidst a joyful celebration, the authorities weren't likely to arrest him and cause a scene.

Nevertheless, when it became clear that people were not only listening to this Jesus of Nazareth but also believing him, the council leaders began to get nervous. Finally, they sent the Temple police.

"Come with us," said the officers, pushing toward Jesus.

"Not yet," he replied. "I'll be here just a little longer, then I'm going back to the one who sent me. After that, if you come looking for me, you won't find me, because you can't go where I'll be going."

Such strange talk! This confused the police. So instead of arresting Jesus, they decided to stick around and listen to some of his preaching. When they finally returned to their leaders — without their prisoner, of course — they were in big trouble.

"Where is this man Jesus?" the leaders demanded. "Why haven't you arrested him?"

The officers could only mumble in awe. "He said such interesting things."

"Speak up! What's the problem?"

"We've never heard anyone preach like he does."

The leaders were enraged. "What's this? Have you been led astray, too? You are police officers. You are supposed to have good sense!"

Then, surprisingly, one of the council elders spoke up. His name was Nicodemus and he had met with Jesus privately on one occasion. "Shouldn't we try him before we convict him?" Nicodemus asked.

Now the leaders were exasperated. One of their own was turning. "What's the matter with you?" they asked, then added sarcastically, "Are you also from Galilee?"

"No," answered Nicodemus. "I only remind you that each of us has two ears. We must hear both sides."

The council members squirmed a little, knowing they had no answer to that. So they hastily adjourned their meeting. Jesus, meanwhile, went on with his preaching.

Now it was the custom that each day of the festival (except the last day) a golden pitcher full of water would be carried to the temple in a ceremonial procession. On the last day of this particular festival, Jesus positioned himself at the entrance to the temple. As always, a crowd gathered around him. He stood there very straight and still until they were quiet, then he said, "If anyone is thirsty, let him come to me and drink."

Once again Jesus had said something very strange — and right in front of the temple! Well, this excited the people more than ever, and, while they were milling about, talking among themselves, Jesus left as quietly as he had come. No cheering or jeering; no good-bye. Just one of the crowd.

Still excited, the people took down their shelters, packed their belongings, and headed for home. This had been the best Festival of Shelters in years! So much to talk about! And the hottest topic of conversation, even though whispered, remained . . . Jesus of Nazareth!

What is this story *really* about?

Celebration:

The Festival of Shelters was a forerunner of "camp meetings." Have you ever been to a camp meeting? What was it like? What are some things your church celebrates?

Controversy:

Jesus was a controversial figure. In what ways was this helpful or harmful to his ministry? Can you name any controversial figures in religion today?

People were afraid to choose sides for or against Jesus. How do you feel about choosing sides?

Freedom:

We enjoy freedom of speech and freedom to assemble. People in Jesus' day didn't have those freedoms. How would you feel if you were threatened with arrest, just because people had gathered around to hear what you had to say? How would you handle the situation?

Let's *talk* about it!

Everyone has heard of Judas Iscariot, one of the Twelve Apostles of Jesus Christ. He was the bad one, the rotten apple in the barrel, the one who betrayed Christ. Let's see, there were Simon Peter and Andrew — come on, help me name them — James and John, Philip and Bartholomew, Matthew and Thomas, James the son of Alphaeus, Thaddaeus, Simon the Patriot, and, of course, Judas.

These were twelve very special people. They were the original disciples, chosen by Jesus Himself. All of us, if we believe in Jesus and follow his teachings, are disciples; but the original twelve had the special title of "Apostle."

What makes the Apostles special? Well, they were given a very specific job to do — not just follow Jesus around like puppy dogs, but carry out God's purpose, which was to save all human beings from their sins. This wasn't a temporary job, either. It was full-time and for life. A BIG job!

So how did Jesus expect twelve people to save the world? Here's an example of how it works: (Use newsprint or chalkboard)

Let's say one Apostle, Thaddaeus, is able to convert five people in his lifetime.

Thaddaeus

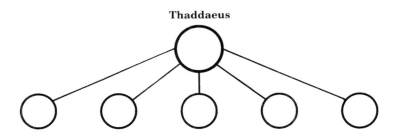

Each of the five then reaches five of his or her own.

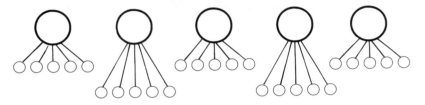

Thaddaeus has now produced thirty new Christians! And if each of the 25 reaches five more, and the five more multiply again, in a very short time Thaddaeus' work will have produced 780 new Christians. Now if all twelve Apostles were equally successful, there would be, in the same amount of time, 9360 new Christians! Just imagine! It's a simple plan, and it's a good plan.

But, one of the apostles, Judas, decided to earn a little extra money by telling the Roman soldiers where Jesus was. He knew that Jesus would be arrested and probably put to death, but still he chose to be a traitor. Maybe the thought of having all that money in his hand was just too much for him. . . . When it was all over, Judas must have been very sorry for what he had done, because he killed himself — right in the middle of the field that he had bought with the betrayal money.

Now there were only eleven Apostles. But Jesus had wanted twelve. . . . Judas had to be replaced. So the eleven called a meeting of about a hundred and twenty believers, or disciples, of Jesus. There were women in the group, of course, including Mary, and Jesus' brothers were there.

Peter conducted the meeting. He said, "The scripture has come true, in which the Holy Spirit, speaking through David, predicted the treachery of Judas. 'Even my best friend,' the scripture says, 'the one I trusted most, the one who shared my food, has turned against me.' It is written in the book of Psalms, 'May someone else take his place of service.' So, then, someone must join us as a witness to the resurrection of the Lord Jesus. He must be one of the men who were in our group during the whole time that the Lord Jesus traveled about with us, beginning from the time John baptized him until the day

116

Jesus was taken up from us to heaven. . . . Whom do you propose?"

They thought about this. Peter had stated two qualifications for the job — experience (one who had been a faithful disciple), and true belief (one who had witnessed the resurrection).

"I propose Joseph Justus," someone said.

"And I propose Matthias," said another.

Both were qualified. "So how shall we decide?" asked Peter.

"The Holy Spirit has helped us in the past," answered one of the women. "He will help us now, if we pray."

So they prayed: "Lord, you know the thoughts of everyone, so show us which of these two you have chosen to serve as an Apostle in the place of Judas Iscariot."

Then they voted, which seems a fair way to choose when all things are equal. The winner was Matthias. And once again there were Twelve Apostles to carry on the Lord's work, to create disciples, to multiply again and again those who would follow the teachings of Jesus. This was the beginning, the seed, of the Christian church as we know it today — this gathering of one hundred and twenty believers who chose the thirteenth Apostle.

What is this story *really* about?

Effectiveness:

All of us would like to make a difference in the world, but we're often defeated by the thought of being only one of billions. If everyone felt that way, would anything ever get accomplished? Remember, each apostle changed hundreds of lives. Each one made a difference — and you can, too!

Democracy:

People voted for the new apostle. Why is voting a good system? They also prayed before voting. What do you suppose would happen if all voters did that today?

Fairness:

The "best man" doesn't always win. How did you feel when you deserved an honor and didn't receive it? How did you react?

Uniqueness:

No one is irreplaceable, as evidenced by the replacement of Judas. Although many may be qualified for the same job, we each bring our own unique personality, talents, and background to shape our work.

Let's *talk* about it!

This is the story of Phoebe, a very special woman who lived in New Testament times. She was Paul's friend. Granted, this story is speculation; nevertheless, there is strong support for the possibility that it happened just this way. What was special about Phoebe?

"Never heard of her," you say.

We know what was special about Mary, or Ruth, or Delilah, even Jezebel. But who was Phoebe?

Well, here's something to think about: If it weren't for Phoebe, we might never have heard that "all have sinned and come short of the glory of God." It's possible that no one would ever have sung, "Behold, I Stand at the Door and Knock." We might never have known that "the wages of sin is death" or that "none is righteous, no, not one."

Have you guessed? Did you recognize Paul's letter to the Romans? . . . Phoebe delivered that letter. And it wasn't easy!

Imagine a loving and trustworthy woman in a long cotton dress, traveling by camel and donkey over the dusty miles through Achaia and Macedonia, then journeying on by boat into the Roman Empire. Add to that a generous measure of self-sufficiency and determination. Call it first century women's lib, if you will — this was no namby-pamby lady!

Travel was difficult and dangerous in those days. No freeways, no airplanes, no policemen or policewomen for protection. No porter carried Phoebe's luggage. And . . . what? She crossed the Sea of Adria without playing shuffleboard?

Paul was worried about her. "I trust you completely, Phoebe," he said, just before she left, "but I am concerned for your safety."

"My safety!" Phoebe answered. "Paul, I live in a seaport. Corinth is full of wickedness. If God were not caring for me, I would already be dead. I have ministered to drunken sailors, degenerate women, escaped murderers, and many just plain irritable people — not to mention you, coming here all tired and ill from those travels of yours. I can certainly manage a journey to Rome!"

Paul couldn't help smiling. No use arguing with her. "Yes," he answered, "I believe you can manage it, Phoebe. And you shall. God will see you through." Then he gave her a note of introduction to the Christians in Rome, so that they would welcome her. And this is what it said. (Pull letter from pocket) . . . I just happen to have a copy!

Dear Friends,

This note will introduce Phoebe, our sister in Christ. She is a deaconess at the church in Cenchreae, a small seaport near Corinth. Please welcome her in the Lord's name, standing together in one spirit and of one mind — that of working together for the faith of the gospel.

Phoebe has been a friend to many people. She is also my friend.

Sincerely,
Paul

So, who was Phoebe? She was Paul's friend; she was the person who delivered his letter to the Romans. She was a hard worker, given to acts of charity and hospitality; she was a good Christian.

Phoebe — mentioned only one time in the entire Bible — was a very special woman!

What is this story *really* about?

Courage:

We all like to think of ourselves as courageous; we picture ourselves as heroes and heroines in action. But when it comes to the real crunch, courage is scarce. Why? Why do people hang back and let "George" do it?

There was no weakness in Phoebe. Why are women referred to as "the weaker sex?" Is this fair?

Commitment:

Sometimes we make commitments but don't follow through. Why should commitment be taken seriously? What are some commitments we make as church members?

Dependability:

It's nice to be called "dependable." It's a wonderful compliment. How do you feel about someone who is not dependable? In what ways do they make life miserable for others?

Let's *talk* about it!

(The story of Phoebe is adapted from *"Five Women, Beautiful Within"* by Janet Litherland. Copyright © 1977, Meriwether Publishing Ltd.)

(Props: A small roll of tape and two cereal boxes. One box is full and intact. The other has been emptied and cut apart at each seam, producing six pieces — top, bottom, and four sides. **Good News Bible,** *optional.)*

(Talk informally with audience. Hold up intact box and invite comments. Do the same with box pieces. Ask if the pieces are a box. Then ask if any one piece by itself is a box.)

Now, if I tape two pieces together (Do it), is this a box? . . . What must I tape together to make a box? (Steer audience toward the correct answer, which is five pieces — bottom and four sides. Quickly tape the five pieces together as you talk with audience.)

What about this other piece, the top? Is it necessary? . . . Okay, the top isn't necessary to call this a box. But, if the box had a top, it would be a better box. Then the cereal would stay fresh, and unwanted critters (roaches) would stay out!

Now let's get personal. Our bodies are made up of many parts — From our heads to our toes,

As the old song goes.

We have hair and we have eyes,

We have hips and we have thighs.

There are ears and there are knees,

Even fingers, if you please!

And think about the parts that hide

Beneath our skin, down deep inside.

Like spine and spleen, and heart and tongue,

And glands and veins, and bones and lungs.

Enough rhyming — it makes me nervous! The point is: A body is made up of many parts. One part alone is not a body. Gee! That sounds like scripture. It sounds like the story the apostle Paul told about what makes a church. . . . First

Corinthians 12:14-22. (Read from *Good News Bible* or memorize the following passage, commenting where appropriate.)

"For the body itself is not made up of only one part, but of many parts. If the foot were to say, 'Because I am not a hand, I don't belong to the body,' that would not keep it from being a part of the body. And if the ear were to say, 'Because I am not an eye, I don't belong to the body,' that would not keep it from being a part of the body. If the whole body were just an eye, how could it hear? And if it were only an ear, how could it smell? As it is, however, God put every different part in the body just as he wanted it to be. There would not be a body if it were all only one part! As it is, there are many parts but one body." (Illustrate) Many pieces. One box.

"So then, the eye cannot say to the hand, 'I don't need you!' Nor can the head say to the feet, 'Well, I don't need you!' On the contrary, we cannot do without the parts of the body that seem to be weaker."

Remember the box top? (Hold it up) It made the box better, even though it wasn't necessary. But there's more to this story than boxes and body parts. Paul tells us in First Corinthians that all of us in this room, even in the world, are like a body. Let's say (pointing) you're the head, you're the legs, and you're the, uh . . . elbows. Each person is important. Yes, even the elbows! If our arms didn't bend at the elbows, how would we feed ourselves?

Again, each person is important. That's how the world works. Imagine a reading class with no teacher — no one would learn to read. Imagine a reading class with no students — no one would learn to read! Sometimes we think we're not necessary, because we're not leaders or organizers, or maybe we're a little shy. We're box tops. Still, if it weren't for us, the cereal would get stale, and the critters (roaches) would take over!

Our church is like that, too. Each person in it is important. Some are teachers, some are students. Some pray out loud and some pray silently. Some do heavy work, like setting up chairs, and some are just plain nice to other people. In order to accomplish God's work, all of us — the "parts" — must be in working order. One of us is not a church, but, taped together, like this box, we can do great things.

What is this story *really* about?

Uniqueness:

One person's strength may be another person's weakness, but each person is special in some way. Sometimes we believe that we have nothing to offer, but no talent or skill or bit of knowledge is too small to use for God.

Cooperation:

Our strengths can compensate for someone else's weaknesses. And the reverse is true, too. One person can't do it all, but together great things can be accomplished. What are some rules to follow so that cooperation will be easy and effective?

Let's *talk* about it!

Saul of Tarsus, who later became Paul, was not one of the original apostles. He said that God made him an apostle, but for a little different reason than that of the other twelve — thirteen, if you count Matthias. Paul said that he was made an apostle so that he might preach the Good News to the Gentiles, while the others were made apostles to the Jews.

This is interesting. Jews and Gentiles did not mix very well in that part of the world at that time. They had racial differences, which extended into their religious life. For Jews, all of life was religious. They followed the law and the customs set forth in the Old Testament; so, even though many became Christians, they still clung to the old ways. Changes were slow and difficult.

Christ had said that all mankind was equal before God, and, by the time Paul and the other Apostles were actively preaching and teaching this message, Jews were worshiping with Gentiles in synagogues. However, they held tightly to the old custom of not eating with Gentiles.

"Let's eat quickly," says the Gentile. "I have business to take care of in the city."

"We do not eat quickly," says the Jew. "Mealtime is for wholesome, leisurely conversation."

"Let's talk about what happened last night," says the Gentile.

"At the table we talk about God," replies the Jew.

"Have some of this," says the Gentile, passing a plate of food.

"Have you tithed it?"

"No."

"Then we would be eating the food of idols," says the Jew, refusing the plate.

"But it's good roast pork," says the Gentile.

"Unclean!" screams the Jew. "Don't you pay any attention to the Holy Scriptures?"

They couldn't agree on much of anything. To the Jewish Christians, mealtime was a time of praise and thanksgiving at God's table. To eat with undisciplined Gentiles would risk contamination. Conservative Christian Jews felt that, as God's chosen people, they should be different, and that it was impossible to be a good Christian without first becoming a Jew and taking up Jewish ways.

The problem with this attitude was that pride and self-righteousness moved in, and equality, which is essential to Christianity, moved out. Customs that separate people are contrary to Christian fellowship. Now if these Jews and these Gentiles could not sit together at an ordinary meal, how, then, could they sit together at the Lord's table for Holy Communion, which is the ultimate expression of Christian fellowship? This was one of the many problems that faced Paul and the other disciples of Christ.

It was in Antioch, the capitol of Syria, that the uniting of all Christians had its best chance of becoming a reality. This was a great commercial city of 500,000 people. It had river access to the Mediterranean and caravan roads entering from the other side. It was set in a valley and shielded by beautiful mountains. Its citizens were aggressive, intelligent, and . . . interracial. It was at Antioch that the first Gentile church was founded, and it was at Antioch that the disciples were first called Christians. Relations between Jews and Gentiles in Antioch were pretty good.

So, when Peter, an apostle to the Jews, went to Antioch, he found a much different, more liberal, atmosphere than what he had been used to in Jerusalem. He was invited to eat with Gentiles. This seemed to be acceptable in Antioch. . . . What should he do? He decided to do as other Antioch Jews were doing and sit at the table.

Peter had eaten several meals with Gentiles when one day some of his friends from Jerusalem arrived. Worried about what they would think of him, he drew back and did not eat with the Gentiles. Some of the Antioch Jews, influenced by Peter's example, backed off, too, including Barnabas, Paul's "right-hand man."

Well, when Paul discovered this, he was furious with Peter and, right in front of everybody, accused Peter of hypocrisy!

There had to have been an argument. These were two very strong Christian men. They were equals. It is unfortunate that we only have access to Paul's opinion, for Paul paints Peter a coward. Was Peter really a coward? Or was he a gentle person doing his best to make everyone a tiny bit happy? Was he trying to be diplomatic? . . . Paul was right in believing very strongly that Christians receive justice by faith in Christ, not by following the law. But was he right to belittle Peter in public? He boasts of it in his letter to the Galatians, making it seem like a good thing to do. What if he had been more discreet? What if he had simply joined the men at the table, setting an example of his own?

Paul picked on Peter. It's recorded in scripture. Did Peter retaliate? We'll never know.

What is this story *really* about?

Stubbornness:

We all like to have our own way. Sometimes we cling fiercely to our "way," even when we know it would be better to give in. What makes us do this? Is it ever okay to be stubborn? When? Why?

Tolerance:

Not all Christians worship God in the same way. What are some differences between Protestants and Catholics? Between Baptists and United Methodists? Between small churches and large churches? Is any one way better than another? How should we Christians treat one another?

Diplomacy:

Peter was trying to "fit in" to both sets of customs. Was this right or wrong? Why? When is it good to be diplomatic? How do people's feelings figure into it?

Let's *talk* about it!

Back in Bible times, a Roman soldier needed a lot of equipment when he went into battle.

Picture this: Over his clothing he wore a breastplate made of bronze to protect his heart. If he were a rich man, he wore, instead, a vest made of chain mail. He also wore a bronze helmet and a pair of greaves, which protected his legs from knee to ankle.

For defense he carried a wooden shield covered with canvas and hide. This was very good against a favorite weapon — arrows that had been tipped with pitch and set on fire — because the arrows would burn themselves out in the tough hide. For offense, the soldier kept a double-edged sword at his thigh and two javelins in his hands.

The soldier would put on all of his equipment except the helmet and sword. The custom was for these two items to be handed to him by someone else.

What a wonderful word picture this makes for the writer of Ephesians to use in urging Christians to "arm" themselves! He does add a belt and shoes to the uniform, and he eliminates the greaves and javelins.

Now imagine yourself as the soldier. You are wearing a breastplate, belt, and greaves. You are carrying a large shield and two light javelins. This time you'll coat the pieces of equipment with "sealer," the powerful stuff that God gives to everyone. It's free!

The belt you'll seal with "truth." This is faithfulness to God's cause.

The breastplate gets a coat of "righteousness," or "right-ness" in character and conduct. This makes you a good person.

Spread a little "peace" on your shoes. "Peace? For going into battle?" Of course, peace. Peace, after all, is the reason for doing battle.

The hide-covered shield you'll seal with "faith," in which the worst, most fiery temptations will burn themselves out!

You won't be able to seal your helmet and sword by yourself, remember, because these sealers are given to you by someone else. You must accept God's salvation to seal your helmet (this gives you his protection) and you must accept his Word to seal your sword (this makes the sword sharp).

Before you go into battle, there is one more thing you'll need — an open line of communication with your superior. Romans soldiers didn't have "walkie-talkies"; they had messengers. The Christian soldier has an even better system. Prayer — open communication with God!

Did you know that God Himself wore "armor" when he rescued his oppressed people? According to Isaiah, "He (God) will wear justice like a coat of armor and saving power like a helmet. He will clothe himself with the strong desire to set things right and to punish and avenge the wrongs that people suffer."

But what was it the early Christians were "arming" themselves against? How did they perceive evil?

More word pictures: Satan was very real. They pictured him as a serpent, a dragon, and as a man with evil characteristics. He had demons, too, and they were considered evil. Then there were fallen angels and other spiritual creatures who worked against God. People also worried about the Roman gods, such as Mercury, Zeus, and Isis. And don't forget the heavenly bodies — moons and stars — that had power over human lives. These people were serious about astrology!

The writer of Ephesians may or may not have believed in these manifestations of evil. We don't know. The important thing is that he realized and appreciated the grip they had on folks. God's armor, sealed with God's power, finally gave the early Christians an opportunity to overcome these evil creatures and take charge of their own lives.

A person dressed up in God's armor was (and still is) a liberated person. . . . Free!

What is this story *really* about?

Protection:

God offers protection to all his children. Why do we need it? What are we being protected from? What must we do to be sure that we have God's protection? It's strange, but not everyone accepts God's offer.

Freedom:

There are two kinds of freedom — "freedom from" and "freedom to." What does this mean?

How can a person, all laced up in God's armor, possibly be FREE?

Let's *talk* about it!

THE MISSION OF EPAPHRODITUS
(Philippians 2:25-30)

Members of the Philippian church were all in a tizzy, especially the women. They had worked for many days on an enormous "care package" for their special missionary, Paul, who was in prison. They had packed clothing, food, little treats and, of course, money. They loved Paul, and there wasn't one of them who didn't want to deliver the package personally. They all wished they could make the long trip from Philippi to Rome but, naturally, this was impossible. There were chores to be done and business to tend to at home.

Who, then, should represent them? Who could take the time to not only deliver the gifts but also to stay with Paul for a while and help him with his missionary work? Work Paul continued to do even from behind bars.

One man fit the bill. His name was Epaphroditus and he was a leader in the Philippian church. Epaphroditus would have the freedom to go and would be an excellent, willing helper for Paul. Excitement soared as everyone fussed over Epaphroditus, getting him ready for the trip. They even made sure his coat was clean and that he had new shoes. My, he looked nice! He certainly lived up to his name — Epaphroditus, you see, was a Greek name that meant "handsome and charming."

So the handsome and charming man set off for Rome, and the people in Philippi didn't hear from him for quite a while, messenger service being what it was in those days.

Then, finally, after what seemed an eternity, a message came. Epaphroditus had arrived safely in Rome, had delivered the wonderful goodies to Paul in prison, and had been working very hard to help Paul with his mission. But . . . somehow, Epaphroditus had become seriously ill, so ill that he had nearly died. . . . And, once again, the Philippians were all in a tizzy, especially the women.

"What if Epaphroditus dies?"

"What if he's unable to continue his work with Paul?"

"What if he's too sick to even come home?"

They fussed so much that word spread all the way to Rome, where Paul and Epaphroditus (who had by this time recovered) heard how distressed the people were. Well, that distress was nothing compared to how this news made Epaphroditus feel. He became distressed over their distress, and this distressed Paul, who decided to take matters into his own hands and clear everything up.

So Paul wrote a letter to the Philippians. Of course it was a long letter of love and concern for them, and it was full of "preachy" things, which they expected of him, but it also told them of Epaphroditus' illness and how God had had pity on him and spared him.

"Not only on him (Epaphroditus) but on me, too," wrote Paul, "and spared me an even greater sorrow." Meaning the sorrow he would have felt had Epaphroditus died.

He also pointed out that Epaphroditus had suffered greatly in the line of duty and that the Philippians should show their gratitude with joy and treat Epaphroditus with the respect he deserved.

Well, Epaphroditus returned to Philippi, delivered the letter, and was very pleased with the way the people received him. They were all in a tizzy again, especially the women. A joyful tizzy, of course. And respectful.

What is this story *really* about?

Being an Ambassador:

Epaphroditus was an ambassador of the Philippian people. He represented them when he took gifts and messages to Paul and when he worked for Paul in place of them. What characteristics make a good ambassador?

We've heard the expression, "an ambassador for Christ." What does this entail?

Concern and Worry:

What is the difference between concern and worry? Neither one is much good unless we act on it. Paul acted on his concern for the Philippian people by sending a letter to alleviate their worry. What can we do to help ourselves when we worry too much?

Let's *talk* about it!

There is a lost city in the New Testament. It is called Colossae, and, at one time, it was a place of great importance. Colossae was a large city, located in the Lycus River Valley, about one hundred miles inland from Ephesus, off the Aegean Sea. It was on the most important trade route from Ephesus to the Euphrates River and was famous for its textiles, particularly a purple-colored wool.

Religiously speaking, Colossae was located in Phrygia, an area known for its cults, its strange prophets, and its odd assortment of gods and goddesses. This made it a particularly difficult place to start a Christian church. Even so, one brave Christian did just that. A Colossian named Epaphras, working under the apostle Paul's direction, evangelized the people of Colossae and organized the Colossian church.

Epaphras was a good pastor, and he battled continually against the influence of the "ancient mysteries." Finally, he took his concerns to Paul, who by now was in a Roman prison. For his trouble, the authorities locked Epaphras up, too.

Paul considered the problem at Colossae and decided that the best thing to do was to send a letter to the Colossian church. His letters at that time were getting out and were being circulated with great success. He labored over this particular letter, and it was a labor of love. Paul had never been to Colossae, yet he had been in constant touch with the people. He felt responsible.

How should he approach the problem of encroaching heresy? This wasn't any ordinary heresy, the kinds he had handled before. It was a local thing, springing from a strange mixture of strict self-denial, which was Jewish in nature, speculation, which was a Greek practice, and the "deep thinking" of the Orientals, which led to weird religious theories. Paul called the whole mixture "the worthless deceit of human wisdom." Whatever it was, it overpowered the simplicity of the gospel. These people were in deep spiritual trouble.

Paul wrote thoughtfully. First he wrote a prayer of supplication and expressed his genuine interest in the people. Then he carefully explained the folly of rituals and mediators and stressed the need for the Gospel. Within this framework, he wrote of the significance of Christ and of the value of the true Christian life. Finally, he gave the people some plain instruction on morals and told them of the importance of prayer. He sent the letter with Tychicus, a friend, and then he waited. . . .

The answer was disappointment. Paul's labor of love did not have the effect he had hoped for. The Colossian church eventually faded and died and, later, the city of Colossae died too. When the road system changed, Colossae lost its importance. During the seventh and eighth centuries it suffered from terrible raids and, finally, its people abandoned it. In the twelfth century the Turks destroyed what was left.

Colossae is a lost city. The only things uncovered by archeologists on its site, hundreds of years later, are the bleak ruins of an ancient church.

No event in Christian history is connected to the city of Colossae. The Apostle Paul never even went there. Colossae died. . . . But because it once lived, you and I have the Book of Colossians — the most devout and elaborately written statement of Christian theology in the New Testament!

What is this story *really* about?

Heresy:

Sometimes strange beliefs and weird practices try to work their way into Christian groups. Sometimes they succeed. Why is this dangerous?

What is a cult? How do cults recruit members? In what ways are cults dangerous?

Attentiveness:

It is one thing to listen; it is another to pay attention. The people of Colossae may or may not have listened to Paul. They certainly didn't pay attention. Do you suppose that the city of Colossae might have survived if its Christian church had not died? How does a church affect a city? How can individual Christians affect their cities?

Let's *talk* about it!

A SCARY THING
(II Thessalonians 2:3-17)

From the beginning of time, human beings have been fascinated — as well as frightened! — by evil. A popular genre of fiction writing today is the horror novel. Folks who read these novels love spooky things; the spookier the better! They love to read about screams and groans, creaking doors, bloody knives, and grotesque figures with sharp teeth and eyes that glow in the dark. In fact, they have great fun being scared to death!

Don't worry. I'm not one of them, and I'm not going to scare you. I am going to tell you, though, about a scary figure in the Bible — even scarier than Satan. . . . What could be scarier than the Devil himself? . . . Let's see, the Devil has been described as the Deceiver, the Great Dragon, the Evil One, the Father of Lies, a murderer, the Old Serpent, the Tempter, the Destroyer, and the Prince of the Powers of the Air, whose consuming passion is to be worshiped. In addition, this powerful, evil devil commands a huge army of wicked spirits who do his bidding! What could be scarier than that?

Listen closely. . . . One of Satan's wicked spirits is waiting . . . has been waiting for thousands of years for his own chance to do evil things. . . . Are you listening? . . . He is a supernatural being in whom the forces of evil are smoldering to the hottest of all temperatures! He has been described as a beast, as a dragon, and as a horrendous monstrous giant. In the Old Testament, Amos and Job refer to him as a sea monster, just waiting to pop out and bite someone! Now that's scary!

Who is this fantastic figure of evil? . . . The apostle, Paul, calls him the Wicked One. He is better known to us as the Antichrist.

"But the Antichrist is just a concept! It is the 'spirit of heresy,' or the 'force of unrighteousness,' or the 'evil spirit' that will tempt us in the last days, which are too far away to even bother about."

You may think that if you like, but that's not what Paul thought. Paul wasn't burdened with our advanced technology and our modern way of thinking. He thought in terms of the times in which he lived. And if he said, "The Wicked One will appear," that's exactly what he meant. Christians of those days believed that the Antichrist would be the physical incarnation of Satan, just as Christ was the incarnation of God.

"The Wicked One," Paul says, "will oppose every so-called god or object of worship and will put himself above them all. He will even go in and sit down in God's Temple and claim to be God." Daniel and Ezekiel in the Old Testament also say that he wants to be God. . . . But the Lord tells this evil person, "You may pretend to be a god, but, no, you are mortal, not divine." (Ezekiel 28:2)

To make things worse, Paul says that the Wicked One will have the power to perform miracles, but that the object of his miracles will be evil and will deceive many people.

At the moment, according to Paul, the Wicked One is being restrained by a mysterious hand. One day, however, before the Second Coming of Christ, this hand will be taken away, and the Wicked One will step out. Will he be a beast or dragon, a sea monster or sharp-toothed giant? Will he look like an angel with a wicked gleam in his glow-in-the-dark eyes? Or, thinking in the terms of our own times — will he come dressed as one of us, so that we won't recognize him for what he really is? . . . What happens if the Antichrist comes next week and we get taken in by his persuasive techniques?

Paul says, "All who have not believed the truth, but have taken pleasure in sin, will be condemned."

That's pretty scary. But there is something we can do to avoid being deceived by the Antichrist: Hold very tightly to the truth of the real Christ.

As for the Wicked One — don't be scared. Wait for the Lord Jesus to blow him away! . . . Well, actually, Paul said that the Lord Jesus would kill him with the breath from his mouth.

139

What is this story *really* about?

Evil:

What is evil? Is it real? Some people believe in "little sins" and "big sins." Is there a difference?

What are some of the ways that Satan uses people? Can we fight Satan? How? How do you believe the Antichrist differs from Satan?

Power:

Everyone has, at some time, enjoyed having power over something or someone. For many people, power is the ultimate goal. Besides wealth, what makes people powerful? Sometimes power is good, and sometimes it's bad.

Let's *talk* about it!

(Note: the storyteller might choose to have Paul's quotes written on a sheet of paper, which could be referred to, as if it were a letter.)

The closing verses of II Timothy give us a unique view of Paul the Apostle. At first glance this passage looks like a list of names and simple instructions, but beyond that we discover a sense of Paul's feelings, his loneliness, and his dependence on his friends.

Paul is in Rome. He is in prison, facing death, and he decides to write a letter to Timothy, his young friend, whom he regards as a son. Timothy is a shy young man and often ill; nevertheless, he is completely faithful and willing to do whatever is asked of him in the name of the Lord. Timothy is pastor of the church in Ephesus when he receives this second letter from Paul, asking him to visit the prison before winter sets in.

Paul begins by saying, "I give thanks to God, as I remember you always in my prayers. . . . I remember the sincere faith you have, the kind of faith that your grandmother Lois and your mother Eunice also had. . . . For this reason I remind you to keep alive the gift that God gave you when I laid my hands on you." This is a very personal letter, all the way through. Paul advises and encourages Timothy and even reminds him to keep out of trouble!

However, at the end of this letter, Paul's thoughts turn inward. "As for me," he writes, "the time has come for me to be sacrificed." He knows he faces death. "Do your best to come to me soon . . . and bring Mark with you."

Then come the final, specific words concerning these men: Demas, Crescens, Titus, Luke, Tychicus, Carpus, and Alexander the metalworker. We know Titus and Luke, and Mark (whom he mentioned earlier), but who were these other people? They must have been important to Paul. . . . Let's explore.

141

Demas was a citizen of Thessalonica and a faithful helper. He and Luke were with Paul at the prison. Luke remained, but Demas had recently left the work, most likely to enter business in Thessalonica. It is possible that he had grown weary of the hardship and danger of a life with Paul. Paul, after all, was perceived as an agitator, and there wasn't much glamor in being his disciple. Paul's letter says, "Demas fell in love with this present world and has deserted me, going off to Thessalonica."

Crescens was probably one of the "seventy-two" chosen by Jesus to precede him to the towns where he would preach. He was practically an "unknown soldier," since his name is only mentioned once in the New Testament. Crescens was faithful to the end, later founding the church at Vienne in Gaul, where he died a martyr. Of him Paul writes, "Crescens went to Galatia, and Titus to Dalmatia." They, apparently, were sent on church business.

Paul also sent Tychicus on a mission. He went to Ephesus. Tychicus was an indispensible behind-the-scenes worker who made it possible for Paul to preach. Tychicus carried letters to the Ephesians and the Colossians, and knew Paul well enough to tell them about his physical condition. He was a man of integrity who had Paul's full confidence. Later, he became a bishop of Colophon . . . and a martyr.

Paul writes to Timothy, "When you come, bring my coat that I left in Troas with Carpus." Troas was a city that Timothy would pass through on his way from Ephesus to Rome, and Carpus had some of Paul's possessions for safe-keeping while Paul was in prison. The coat would have been a coarse, wool, blanket-like covering with a hole in the middle for the head to go through. It was used as protection against the weather. Winter was coming on, after all, and the prison would be cold and damp.

Paul had also left books and parchments with Carpus, and Timothy was asked to bring those too, *especially the parchments*. Books of that time were rolls of papyrus. They would help pass the time and strengthen the mind. Parchment was a very expensive writing material, and we know that Paul did a great deal of writing. Especially the parchments, he had said. Carpus must have been a valued friend to have been entrusted with these possessions. Later, Carpus became bishop of Berytus in Thrace. He, too, was martyred.

Alexander the metalworker was not one of Paul's companions. Alexander was a Christian, but a dissenter — one whose views were opposed to the accepted church doctrine. As far as Paul was concerned, he was a trouble-maker, and Paul's bitterness seems to be personal. It's possible that Alexander had been a hostile witness at Paul's trial. He had already been excommunicated from the church, but he was still a very influential man, and Timothy was warned to stay out of his way. Paul quotes Psalms 62:12 when he writes, "The Lord will reward him (meaning Alexander) according to what he has done."

Paul is lonely:

"Do your best to come to me soon. Get Mark and bring him with you."

Paul is also doing something very human, something all of us do from time to time — he is feeling sorry for himself:

"No one stood by me the first time I defended myself. All deserted me."

He knows he is going to die:

"The time is here for me to leave this life."

But, despite his sadness and his melancholy mood, he feels good about his work:

"I have done my best in the race, I have run the full distance, and I have kept the faith."

Of the eight men mentioned by Paul in this letter, one worked against him, one left him, and six remained faithful. Of these six, five were martyred. We don't know what became of Titus.

No one ever said Christianity would be easy. It wasn't easy then . . . and it's not easy now. But there is, according to Paul's letter, "a prize of victory awarded for a righteous life —

the prize which the Lord will give to all those who wait with love for him to appear."

. . . Paul waited. With love.

What is this story *really* about?

Loneliness:

Paul had been in prison for quite a while. He wasn't a thief or a murderer. He was a political prisoner, in prison for doing what he thought was right. He was lonely. We, too, get lonely from time to time, even when there are lots of people around. How is this possible? What can be done about it? How can we become more aware of loneliness in other people?

Friendship:

Name some things you like about your best friend. Paul liked to keep in touch with his friends. Why is this important? Sometimes friendships are broken beyond repair.

Feeling Good About Yourself:

It isn't wrong to feel good about something you've done — it's natural. Boasting about it is what's wrong. There's a difference between accepting a compliment graciously and bragging about your achievements. What are some ways we can improve our self-esteem without becoming big-headed?

Let's *talk* about it!

This is the story of Titus, the man whose name appears on top of the seventeenth book of the New Testament. If the story seems incomplete, it's beause the information passed to us through the centuries is incomplete. It is, however, enough to give us a clear picture of a remarkable person.

Titus was a Greek, born of Gentile parents. We don't know anything about his early years, but we do know that he was converted to Christianity by Paul and that they were as close as brothers. Titus was a strong person, both in body and in spirit, and was able to give the apostle Paul moral support and comfort when he needed them most.

One huge problem that Paul faced in his ministry was getting the Jewish Christians and Gentile Christians together. To agree on things. Anything! Jewish Christians clung fiercely to the old customs and rules of their ancestors. That's understandable. But they also insisted that Gentiles adopt their customs, including circumcision, when converted to Christianity. In other words, become like them.

This outraged the Gentiles. "That's against the message of Christ!" they cried. "Don't you know that anyone can come to Jesus on faith alone? Even Gentiles!"

Paul's patience and diplomacy were tested time and again by the bickering of these two groups, but nothing caused as much trouble as the problem of circumcision. This was a Jewish custom and the Christian Jews insisted it was necessary for Gentiles, too, if they wanted to be Christian. Paul dealt with it as best he could.

Then along came Titus, Paul's personal convert and personal friend . . . and Titus refused to be circumcised! It was time for a "test case." The two men agreed to stick together and, finally, with Paul's powers of persuasion, Titus was accepted as a member of the Christian community — without circumcision. This was extremely important, because it set a precedent for cases that followed. It was especially useful to the Galatians, when their turn came to argue against circumcision.

Titus, at some point, started a ministry in Corinth. Later, he left it in what he thought were good hands and moved on to another city. But things fell apart. The Corinthian Christians got restless and began to fuss among themselves. Rumors reached Paul that they were ignoring his instructions and were even questioning his leadership. So Titus and Paul developed a plan: Titus would go to Corinth, where he was known, and see if the rumors were true. Paul would also travel toward Corinth, but more slowly, so that he could intercept Titus on the return trip. They would then talk about what Titus had found out and decide what to do. A real first century "intelligence operation!"

As it turned out, some of the rumors were true. But Titus, being the capable and trusted leader he was, straightened things out, so that when he met Paul in Macedonia, the report was good. It lifted Paul's spirits considerably!

Titus, apparently, had a real knack for cleaning up sticky situations. At the time of Paul's letter to Titus (the New Testament book), Titus was beginning a ministry in Crete as supervisor of several very disobedient churches. According to Paul, the Cretans were "liars, wicked beasts, and lazy gluttons" and their church leaders were men "who rebel and deceive others with their nonsense." Imagine walking into a job like that!

Now Titus probably didn't need much advice, but Paul felt obliged to give it to him anyway. Or maybe Paul felt he was returning some moral support, which Titus had given him so often in the past. In either case, Paul's letter reads like a "how-to" manual:

1. How to clean up congregational life.

2. How to clean up home life.

3. How to clean up social life.

Titus' job in Crete was an enormous one, but he did it and did it well. Titus, a Gentile convert and Paul's personal friend,

146

the "test case" on the problem of circumcision, the diplomat and mediator for the quarreling Corinthians, and the "clean-up" man for the mess in Crete, made himself nearly indispensable to Paul the apostle.

Titus was later recognized as the first bishop of the Cretan church.

What is this story *really* about?

Mediation:

Titus was a mediator. He listened patiently to arguments; he worked out solutions. Not everyone has this ability. Often it's difficult for us to look at both sides of an issue, because we only want to look at one side.

I Timothy 2:5 says, "For there is one God, and one mediator between God and men, the man Christ Jesus." What does that mean?

Let's *talk* about it!

This is the story of Philemon and Onesimus, but mostly of Onesimus, a lowly slave who one day became a respected bishop of a Christian church.

Onesimus was a young man — a very bright and talented young man, which was why he was captured and sold into slavery. He could bring a high price!

It happened that he was purchased by a man named Philemon, a wealthy Christian in whose home the Colossian church held its services. It was here that Onesimus, listening through doors, first learned of Christianity, though he was a long way from becoming a Christian himself. In fact, he did a very unchristian thing — he robbed his master, Philemon, and ran away. Onesimus didn't believe this was wrong, because he believed with all of his heart that he had been victimized, not by Philemon, who was a kind master, but by those who had sold him into a life he felt he did not deserve. Remember, this was a smart young man. He thought he deserved better than slavery, and he meant to free himself from it any way he could.

In those days runaway slaves, if they were re-captured, were always flogged, sometimes killed. This was a serious crime. Onesimus was lucky, because someone from the Colossian church recognized him on the streets of Rome and persuaded him to visit the apostle, Paul, in prison.

Well, after just one visit, Onesimus found he could not stay away. Paul's message of Jesus Christ drew him back again and again until finally, one day, he fell on his knees and wept for joy, receiving the love of Christ into his own life. Onesimus then became important to Paul, much like a son, filling his lonely days, delivering messages, and working as often as he was able under the circumstances.

"Onesimus," Paul said one day, "I wish I could keep you with me. You would be a great help in spreading the Good News. Your name means 'useful,' you know."

Onesimus grinned his pixie grin. He knew he hadn't been especially useful to Philemon, mostly on purpose, and Paul knew it too. But he was determined to be useful in the future. He was a Christian now. . . . But then he realized that Paul was thinking of sending him back to Philemon. What possible use could he be as a slave?

"Let me stay and work with you, Paul," he begged. "There is so much I can do for you and for our Lord!"

Paul considered this. He really did. Why send a good man back into slavery? Why give him menial tasks when he could become a minister of the gospel? Besides, Philemon didn't honestly need Onesimus. Paul did. Oh, he was tempted, all right! He was torn between what he wanted to do and what he should do. In the end, Paul decided that the only honorable thing to do was send Onesimus back to Philemon. But . . . he would write Philemon a letter that would not only ask for kindness and understanding on Onesimus' behalf, it would also hint at his (Paul's) own wishes. Ah! He was a crafty one!

(Read from copy of letter)

"Dear Philemon," he writes, "and Apphia, and Archippus, and the church that meets at your house."

Think about that. Since the letter was addressed to all those people, Philemon couldn't keep its contents to himself. He had to share the letter with other Christians, who would undoubtedly want to help Paul's cause.

"This letter," Paul continues, "comes to you from Paul, a prisoner for the sake of Jesus Christ, and from our brother Timothy."

Not just from Paul, but from Timothy also! Now who could deny a request from two such formidable men?

"I could be bold enough," he says, "as your brother in Christ, to order you to do what should be done. But because I love you, I make a request instead." Some request!

149

"I am sending Onesimus back to you now," he continues, "and with him goes my heart. I would like to keep him here with me while I am in prison . . . however . . . I will not do anything unless you agree." Now that's quite a hint!

Paul also promises to pay Philemon, personally, for anything that Onesimus owes. He ends his plea this way: "I am sure, as I write this, that you will do as I ask — in fact I know that you will do even more."

Imagine Philemon reading this letter to his congregation. Would it be possible, then, to turn down Paul's request? Not likely! Poor Philemon didn't stand a chance.

This is the end of Paul's letter to Philemon, but is there more to the story of Onesimus? Probably so.

Our first clue is that the letter — a personal letter containing no lessons or sermons — was saved and included among Paul's published works. It is reasonable to assume, then, that Onesimus was sent back to Paul.

Our second clue occurs in the writings of Ignatius, who was bishop of Antioch in Syria. He tells of a man named Onesimus, bishop of the church at Ephesus. The time frame is right.

If Philemon's Onesimus had, indeed, been returned to Paul and had become one of his assistants — a minister of the gospel — it is very likely that such a bright and enterprising person would eventually become an important leader in the Christian church.

There is no proof of this, but many respected theologians hold to this theory. It makes an interesting story: From slave to bishop.

One thing is certain — Onesimus was "useful." When Christians make themselves useful, anything is possible!

What is this story *really* about?

Injustice:

Slavery is an injustice — Onesimus was a victim. Onesimus stole money from a "just" master and ran away —

Philemon was a victim. How do we decide what is "just" and what is "unjust," what is equitable and fair? Was Onesimus' running away justified? If so, how?

Paul was unjustly imprisoned. How do you feel about that? And Paul sent Onesimus back into slavery. Was that justified? How did Paul redeem the situation?

What can we, as Christians, do to fight injustice in the world?

Usefulness:

Sometimes we Christians just sit on our hands and say, "I'm a Christian." We don't put our Christianity to good use. If we aren't useful Christians, we aren't much.

Let's *talk* about it!

(The story of Onesimus is adapted from *"Five Men, Touched by God"* by Janet Litherland. Copyright © 1978 by Meriwether Publishing Ltd.)

Just exactly how did a young man in Bible times become a priest or a high priest? Notice I said man. Women of Bible times, of course, did not enjoy the equal status of today's women.

The writer of Hebrews tells us of two paths leading to the priesthood. We're going to follow a young man down one of these paths. Let's say his name is Zachary. We'll call him Zach.

Zach, like young people throughout time, thought a lot about what he wanted to become. He'd thought of training to be a doctor or a soldier, and had seriously considered becoming a tiller or as we say today — a farmer. His father and his grandfather before him made a good living being tillers. But Zach believed that he had spiritual gifts that could be put to better use. He was patient and kind, he loved to work with people — he could envision himself helping them with their problems — and he had a special talent for teaching and speaking. He became aware of this talent when neighborhood children returned to him again and again to hear his stories — stories he had learned from the scriptures.

"I want to become a priest," he said one day to his father.

"A priest? You want to become a priest? Not a tiller like your father and your grandfather?"

"No, sir. A priest," replied Zach. "I believe I have special gifts."

"Well, now," said his father, slowly. He scratched his head. "I suppose your brothers could work the land without you. . . . A priest, you say?"

"Yes, sir."

"Hmmmm. . . ." Zach's father looked out across the soil his family had tended for so many years. "My son, the priest," he said finally. "I suppose I could get used to the idea."

Zach was elated. Having his father's support and encouragement was very important to him. Even necessary. So Zach and his father went to the Temple, where first they prayed, then visited with the old Temple priest.

Zach was told that he must meet certain qualifications to attain the priesthood:

1. He must be a Levite. All priests were descended from Aaron of the tribe of Levi. (That was no problem. Zach's family was Levite.)

2. He must be committed to working for the good of men and the glory of God. (Zach was.)

3. He must be willing to offer gifts freely and to make sacrifices for his own sins, even though he was to strive for a sinless life. (Zach certainly recognized the importance of this.)

4. He must have patience and compassion and be willing to teach those in need of learning. (Zach had already recognized this characteristic in himself.)

5. He must suffer, so that he could develop strength and be sympathetic to fellow sufferers. (This, Zach would have to experience.)

6. He must pray often and fervently with tears and cries to God, that he would overcome weakness and temptation. (This, too, Zach would have to work on.)

After much discussion it was agreed that Zach might be a good candidate for the priesthood, but he would have to work hard to prove himself. Even then, his priesthood would not be assured.

"You would have to be appointed," said the old priest. "You cannot seize the office for yourself, nor can you purchase it. Do you understand what is ahead of you, my son?"

Zach understood — many years of hard work and no guarantees! But he was determined to do it. He believed God had called him. (If Zach had been born in a priest's home, his path would have been much easier. He would have been trained from childhood and would have become a priest, whether he wanted to or not.)

There was another rule concerning the priesthood, which was not discussed with Zach, simply because it did not apply: A king could not be a priest, could not tend to "holy matters." King Saul tried it. He burned sacrifices and was severely reprimanded by Samuel. King Uzziah fared even worse. He tried to perform priestly duties and was given leprosy for his trouble!

Now let's shift mental gears for a moment. The scriptures refer several times to Jesus as "High Priest." Let's see if, through the writer of Hebrews, we can track his qualifications.

Was Jesus a Levite? . . . No. He came from the tribe of Judah — a tribe never mentioned in connection with priests.

Was he appointed by his fellow men? . . . No. He was sworn in by God Himself who declared him "a priest forever, in the priestly order of Melchizedek."

Wait a minute! Who in the world is Melchizedek? . . . Old Testament writers mention him very sparingly and with good reason — they were embarrassed by him, because he was both a priest and a king! Not only that, there were no records of his birth, no proof that he was a Levite. Still, he was a priest who was respected by Abraham, the founder of the Hebrew nation and of Judaism. Abraham, whom the apostle Paul had called "the father of all who believe," had accepted bread and wine and blessings from Melchizedek and had paid tithes to him.

So Jesus, who could not be a priest through the accepted Levite chain, would be High Priest "after the order of Melchizedek," the priest-king with no birth records, the old priest who had been swept under the rug! It was clear that if Jesus Christ were really High Priest, some changes were in store for the priesthood.

How did Jesus qualify?

1. He met human need. Quoting St. Francis of Assisi: "Where there is despair — hope" (That's Christ);

"Where there is darkness — light; where there is sadness — joy."

2. Jesus was holy, or sinless.

3. Since he had no sin, he had no guilt and, therefore, had no need to offer sacrifices. (Though he did offer the ultimate sacrifice: Himself.)

4. He was exalted above the heavens.

5. Most important, his appointment by God (his "calling") superceded the law.

Earthly priests, or ministers, serve an important function, but they never quite satisfy our hunger for God. . . . Jesus does!

So, how can you become a priest or minister these days? Same way as in the olden days — by being called of God, as Zach and Jesus were; by working very hard, as Zach and Jesus did; and by understanding that there are no guarantees . . . except that God will hold your hand.

What is this story *really* about?

Calling:

What does it mean to be "called" by God? Aren't all Christians "called?" How is a minister's calling different? Think about special qualities you admire in a favorite minister or priest. Are these just "ministerial" qualities, or do all Christians have them?

The ministry has been described as a "hard life." Do you suppose this is true? Why or why not?

Faith:

Faith is essential to the Christian life — not just believing in God, but believing in what he can do. Even more, it's believing in what he can do through you.

Let's *talk* about it!

Teaching has always been considered a noble profession. A good teacher not only has knowledge and a competent means of presenting it; he or she also feels a sense of responsibility to the students. "Teacher" is a title of respect. It was the same in Bible times.

Paul ranked teachers just below apostles and prophets. That's a pretty high ranking! Back then, teaching and religion were interwoven, because teaching was usually done in churches and synagogues. The teacher held a position of high honor and great moral responsibility. In addition to teaching the "basics" for everyday living, the teacher supervised theological discussion, raising issues and answering questions about such things as Holy Days, sacraments, and interpretation of scripture. Since this was considered a full-time job, local congregations paid the wages.

James, the author of one of our New Testament books, was such a teacher. He was a good, commonsense, moral man. He wasn't particularly "deep," that is, overly concerned with difficult spiritual problems; rather, James was most concerned with day-to-day conduct. He wanted to help people cope with immediate problems. For example, if a hungry person came to James for help, James would feed him first, then tend to spiritual things. His philosophy was that a person who is physically comfortable is a better listener or student.

Like all good teachers, James chose teaching techniques that worked best for him. His favorite seems to be the "diatribe." This is a lively debate with an imaginary opponent. It works like this:

1. Quote the opponent's argument.
2. Discredit the argument.
3. Appeal to the listeners for agreement.

James' most famous lesson, in diatribe form, concerns faith and works. It begins with the example of the hungry person.

First, the opponent's argument:

"My brothers, what good is it for someone to say that he has faith if his actions do not prove it? Can that faith save him?"

Second, discrediting the argument:

"Suppose there are brothers and sisters who need clothes and don't have enough to eat. What good is there in your saying to them, 'God bless you! Keep warm and eat well!' — if you don't give them the necessities of life?"

Third, expecting agreement:

"So it is with faith: if it is alone and includes no actions, then it is dead."

Immediately, he sets up another diatribe:

"But someone will say, 'One person has faith, another has actions.' My answer is 'Show me how anyone can have faith without actions. I will show you my faith by my actions.' . . . Do you want to be shown that faith without actions is useless? How was our ancestor Abraham put right with God? It was through his actions, when he offered his son Isaac on the altar. Can't you see? His faith and his actions worked together; his faith was made perfect through his actions. And the scripture came true that said, 'Abraham believed God, and because of his faith God accepted him as righteous.' And so Abraham was called God's friend. . . . It was the same with the prostitute Rahab. She was put right with God through her actions, by welcoming the Israelite spies and helping them to escape by a different road. You see, then, that it is by his actions that a person is put right with God, and not by his faith alone."

That's pretty persuasive. James even used colorful examples. Perhaps he also used charts and drew illustrations as he taught. He certainly made excellent use of imagery. For example:

"A ship, big as it is and driven by such strong winds, can be steered by a very small rudder."

Or this one:

"Just think how large a forest can be set on fire by a tiny flame!"

Or, best of all:

"Man is able to tame and has tamed all other creatures — wild animals and birds, reptiles and fish. But no one has ever been able to tame the tongue . . . . We use it to give thanks to our Lord and Father and also to curse our fellow-man. . . . No spring of water pours out sweet water and bitter water from the same opening. A fig tree cannot bear olives; a grapevine cannot bear figs, nor can a salty spring produce sweet water."

James was an excellent teacher. He loved his work and treated it with great respect. Likewise, he, the teacher, was treated with great respect.

What is this story *really* about?

Respect for Teachers:

Most teachers are overworked and underpaid. Many work in overcrowded school districts that lack adequate funding, so their classes are too large and their supply of materials is too short. Many students are ungrateful and disrespectful. Still, good teachers hang in there, trying their best to teach. Why do they do it? What are some indications that a person is a good teacher? What are some things that we could do to show teachers that we really appreciate them?

Respect for Work:

Jobs are not always easy to get. Sometimes there are too many engineers, too many beauticians, or too many of something else, and people have a difficult time finding employment. Some folks who have good jobs don't do their work well — they just do enough to collect a paycheck. James, of the New Testament, had great respect for his work as a teacher and did his job very well. Why is it important to respect your work? What are some rewards that a person gets, other than a paycheck, for doing his or her job well?

Let's *talk* about it!

Last night's TV news included a lengthy — and rather enlightening! — eyewitness report. The reporter, Peter Simon, had apparently been following a certain radical movement for a long time. First, he gave the audience some background information. We all know that the biggest newsmaker was a traveling preacher named Jesus of Nazareth. His preaching and teaching were so effective that he has been hailed by much of the world as the promised Messiah and has, indeed, performed miracles — and continues to do so. Our reporter has been an eyewitness to many of them. It has also been established that Jesus of Nazareth was crucified, that he was buried, and that he came back to life. Peter Simon also witnessed these events—even the miraculous resurrection of Jesus from the dead.

But, now let us bring Mr. Simon's story to the present. Many years have passed, and the proclaimed Messiah's promise of a return to earth has not taken place. Was this Jesus of Nazareth, in fact the Messiah? If so, why hasn't he kept his promise to his followers, now scattered over a large area of the world? The true Messiah would certainly be capable of keeping promises.

Some of the general population has been raising that very question and, last night, caused a great deal of trouble with their scoffing attitude. It seems there was a rally in the streets near the Temple. Because of the large number of people, police were conspicuously present. There were pickets and banners and a lot of shouting and chanting, which led our reporter to ask the age-old question: Why?

He approached a man who was waving a banner that read, "Jesus didn't practice what he preached! Look for another Messiah!"

"Why do you care whether Jesus of Nazareth keeps his promises?" asked Mr. Simon.

160

"Because my brothers and their families gave up good livings to 'spread the gospel,' as they call it," answered the man. "Not only them — other friends have wasted their lives, and for what? Nothing changes! Everything is still the same as it was since the creation of the world! I want Christians to see this man from Nazareth for what he was — a man — and then come home while there's some life left to live!"

Peter Simon turned to a young man who was chanting something incomprehensible. "Excuse me, sir," he said. "What is it you're chanting?"

"Christians are a silly lot, Christians are a silly lot!" he replied rhythmically, his mouth moving closer to the microphone.

"Your reason for saying that?" asked the reporter.

"Science, Bud," replied the man. "Science shows that Christianity is absurd. Have you seen any evidence to prove what Christians teach? Any at all?"

"Well, yes, as a matter of fact, I have," began Mr. Simon. . . . But the young man had already turned away, intent on his chant. "Christians are a silly lot, Christians are a silly lot!"

Then our reporter spotted an old woman standing slightly apart from the crowd. She carried no pickets or banners, and she wasn't chanting; but her body swayed from side to side, caught up in the rhythm of the moment.

"Ma'am?" Peter Simon said, approaching her. "Would you mind answering a few questions for our television audience?"

She looked warily at the microphone, then sighed and shrugged.

"Why are you here?" the reporter asked.

"I came to listen," she said. "I need to decide if I really am a crazy old woman."

"Ma'am? . . . I don't understand."

The camera caught the sadness in her eyes as she turned to Peter Simon. "I'm a Christian," she replied. "At least I'm supposed to be. Lately, though, I've wondered if all these years I've given in service might have been better spent."

"How do you mean?" asked the reporter, gently.

The woman sighed. "For many years I've believed in the promises of Jesus, especially the Second Coming. I've waited, even hoped for it. Yet I've seen an entire generation pass before my eyes, and nothing happens. To tell you the truth, I'm beginning to lose interest."

"But, Ma'am, don't you think we should give the Messiah a little more time?"

"Time?" The woman raised her voice. "Jesus said 'the time is near.' He said that more than once."

Peter Simon backed off. The woman's attitude had shocked him, even though he had expected it. Now he needed a few moments to gather his thoughts and prepare his closing remarks — you know how reporters always "sum up" things. His words, he knew, must be strong, swift, and . . . persuasive. This is no "unbiased" reporter, you see. This reporter is an energetic, devoted Christian. As it happens, the TV station for which he reports is Christian-owned and allows, even encourages, his comments. Fortunately, Peter Simon is the type of reporter-commentator who really listens to people before he responds.

"Ladies and gentlemen, this is Peter Simon reporting from the Temple area of the city," he began. The camera moved in for a close-up.

"Many people have gathered to ridicule Christians and to test their beliefs. We knew this would happen. Jesus himself predicted it.

"They ask: 'He promised to come, didn't he? Where is he? Our fathers have already died, but everything is still the same as it was since the creation of the world!' They purposely ignore the fact that long ago God gave a command, and the heavens and earth were created. The earth was formed by water, and it was also by water, the water of the flood, that the old world was destroyed. . . . Do not forget one thing — there is no difference in the Lord's sight between one day and a thousand years; to him the two are the same. The Lord is not slow to do what he has promised, as some think. Instead, he is patient, because he does not want anyone to be destroyed, but wants all to turn away from their sins. (II Peter 3:4-9)

"My colleagues and I have not depended on made-up stories in making known to you the mighty coming of our Lord Jesus Christ. With our own eyes we saw his greatness. We were there when he was given honor and glory by God the Father, when the voice came to him from the Supreme Glory, saying, 'This is my own dear Son, with whom I am pleased!' We ourselves heard this voice coming from heaven, when we were with him on the holy mountain. We were eyewitnesses. (II Peter 1:16-18)

"Jesus of Nazareth was a man whose divine authority was clearly proven to you by all the miracles and wonders which God performed through him. You yourselves know this, for it happened here among you. You, too, were eyewitnesses. (Acts 2:22)

"These things should make us confident of the message proclaimed by the prophets. You will do well to pay attention to it, because it is like a lamp shining in a dark place until the day dawns and the light of the morning star shines in your hearts. . . . (II Peter 1:19) This is Peter Simon, reporting live from the Temple."

I wanted to share Peter Simon's report with you, because it means everything to me. Even though I was safely tucked away at home in front of my TV set last night, I was one of those faltering Christians he talked about. Now, however, I am going to renew my dedication to God and wait for what he has promised — new heavens and a new earth, where righteousness will be at home. I am going to be on my guard, so that I will not be led away by the errors of lawless people and fall from my safe position. (II Peter 3:13,17)

Peter Simon is not only a good reporter and interesting commentator, he is a righteous man, and I respect his opinions. He said to pay attention. . . . I'm paying attention!

What is this story *really* about?

Promises:

A promise is as good as the person who makes it. What does that mean? Each of us, at some time, has been the victim of a broken promise. Remembering how it felt should make us think twice about breaking one ourselves. Why is it important to keep promises?

Patience:

Peter says, "The Lord is not slow to do what he has promised. Instead, he is patient, because he does not want anyone to be destroyed." Have you ever thought about that before? Think about it now. . . . Did you realize that "one day and a thousand years" are the same to the Lord? . . .

It's hard for us, sometimes, to be patient with other people, especially those closest to us. What is there about the world we live in that makes patience a hard thing to achieve? How can we teach ourselves to become more patient?

Let's *talk* about it!

DIOTREPHES BEHAVES BADLY
(III John 9-12)

In the early days of the Christian church, the gospel message was spread from place to place by traveling Christians. These Christians also delivered personal letters and current news. There were no radios or TV sets, no newspapers or telephones, and no computers with convenient modems. So the visits of these traveling Christians (missionaries, street preachers) were welcomed by all people in the communities, not just by church folk. These visits meant news, some excitement, something different!

Though there was an occasional inn for spending the night, Christian travelers did not have access to an abundance of motels and hotels, nor money to pay for them if they had existed. Instead, they depended on "bed and breakfast," freely provided by other Christians. Traditionally, travelers did not accept hospitality from those to whom they preached — the unbelievers — because they didn't want anyone to think that they preached only to receive room and board. They wanted people to listen to their gospel messages free of charge, knowing that the only motive was the message itself. This was a good system.

Unfortunately, there were some evangelists in those days, just as there are in modern days, who abused the system. They accepted, even solicited, money and hospitality from unbelievers for their own gain. Some also pressured the Christians for hospitality, simply to save themselves money. All of these borderline bunco artists were called "false prophets."

It is important to understand that, for the Christians, providing hospitality was not an option — it was a duty. It was an opportunity to take part in the spreading of the gospel. Christians were also instructed by the Elders to give to anyone in need, even strangers. Of course it was difficult to weed out the "false prophets," so charitable Christians were often victims. They were deceived and taken advantage of.

The Apostle John tells about a church leader who fought this abuse of the system but went a little too far. He got so carried away with his own importance that he became an abuser himself. His name was Diotrephes.

Diotrephes was a new-generation church leader. He was ambitious and enjoyed the power of his position. He also had developed a lot of newfangled ideas that were a bit out of step with the old ways. Consequently, his attitude toward authority of the Elders — toward John and the other Apostles who had, for the most part, turned over the work to younger men — was one of contempt. Diotrephes knew better than they did!

And this is what he knew: He could keep false prophets out of his church. It was very simple — just keep all travelers out! So he barred the doors and hung up signs and preached to his own congregation. And the more he preached, the more radical he became, touting his righteousness and demanding compliance with his wishes. Not content to lift up himself, he belittled the old apostles and their work. Still, he didn't become truly malicious until some of his church members defied his orders and offered hospitality to strangers. This he would not tolerate! Screaming from the pulpit, he again forbade them to offer assistance to anyone and threatened them with excommunication if they disobeyed — not just excommunication from the local church, but from the church in general. In other words, Diotrephes awarded himself the power of a bishop!

It was time for the church Elders to step in. In fact, the apostle John decided to pay Diotrephes a personal visit. The Scriptures do not record the meeting between these two men, but it is clear that John approached it with reason and confidence. He was sure he could straighten things out.

Diotrephes had become an obstacle to the progress of the Christian church. It is possible that there were theological differences between his Elders and him just as there are various doctrines and beliefs among Christians today. Nevertheless, Christian charity is universal and should transcend differences.

"Do not imitate what is bad," John said, meaning Diotrephes, "but imitate what is good."

What is this story *really* about?

Abuse of Power:

"False prophets" of Bible times abused their power by taking advantage of the people they preached to. Are "false prophets" operating in the world today? What do they do? How should they be dealt with? Diotrephes was a good man gone bad. He meant well, at first. But it's easy to get carried away with an idea that has taken root in your mind or heart. Even a good idea, taken to extremes, loses its goodness.

Self-importance:

Diotrephes had a large measure of self-importance. How does this differ from self-esteem? What are the consequences of being self-important?

Let's *talk* about it!

According to the scriptures, Jesus had earthly brothers — James, Joseph, Judas (or Jude) and Simon (Mark 6:3). He also had several sisters, but we don't know their names.

Many good Bible scholars believe that Jude, the author of the book of Jude, was the earthly brother of Jesus. We'll assume this is true.

Both Jude and his brother, James, refer to themselves in their New Testament letters as servants of Christ rather than as brothers of Jesus or even as "brothers in Christ," a phrase widely used by other Christians. This indicates that both were deeply humble men, utterly devoted. . . . They were servants.

Jude had come a long way. Growing up with Jesus in the household of Joseph and Mary, he had little interest in his brother's ministry or in his claim to be the Messiah. Like any young person, the attention focused on his older bother sometimes annoyed him. It wasn't until after the Resurrection that Jude finally believed and became a true disciple. In some ways it's a pity — he missed so much! But maybe it worked out for the best. Maybe his many years of unbelief, and possibly regrets, strengthened his devotion, made it more poignant.

Jude's letter was written to Christians everywhere — even to me and to you. When he first sat down to write, he intended to compose a nice, straightforward letter about the faith and about the salvation that all of us as Christians share. In fact, he had written several paragraphs when suddenly he changed his mind. He tore up his scribblings, tossed them away, and started over.

Something worried Jude — something that had been going on in Christian churches — and it had gnawed at him until he could ignore it no longer. This "something" was far more important than his original message. Preachers do that

168

all the time, you know — change their sermons — especially when a situation calls for immediate attention.

Jude's writing is fresh, original, and very picturesque, as he describes what is in his heart. . . . Let's have him tell you, in his own words.

(Pause. Change position, assume the character of Jude, and proceed as a monolog.)

My friends . . . I am deeply disturbed. Some godless people have slipped in unnoticed among us. You knew this would happen, because the Apostles predicted it. I am only reminding you to be watchful, so that you aren't deceived and swept into unbelief. Remember, for your own sakes, that God has no patience with those who turn away from him. . . . Remember that he once rescued the people of Israel from Egypt, but afterward destroyed those who did not believe; remember the angels who strayed and are now bound with eternal chains; remember Sodom and Gomorrah, whose immoral people now suffer the punishment of eternal fire.

Am I trying to scare you? . . . Yes! If we Christians do not hold fast to our faith, Judgment will be a terrible day for us!

Let me tell you what to watch for: These people are always grumbling and blaming others; they are self-centered; they are parasites, clinging to people of wealth and prestige; and they will flatter you to get their own way. What concerns me most is that these heretics are successful! Working from within the church, their power is alarming!

Let me scare you a little more. . . . There are some things about these people that you may not know, may not even suspect:

Did you know that they have visions which make them sin against their own bodies? They believe that religion is spiritual only, that it has nothing to do with life in the flesh, with morality. They can freely indulge their whims. Therefore, they may be lustful and perverted, or outrageously indecent, with no concern for their fellow man. They use the grace of God as license to sin!

169

Did you know that these heretics despise God's authority and insult the glorious beings above? Not even the archangel Michael did this to the Devil himself! When the Devil wanted to bury Moses, claiming that Moses' body belonged to him as lord of the material world, Michael simply said, "The Lord rebuke you." He did not cast insults at a supernatural being.

Did you know that these heretics accept money for turning people away from the Lord?

My friends,

These people are like dirty spots in your fellowship meals.

They are like rainless clouds and fruitless trees.

They are like wild waves of the sea, with their shameful deeds showing up like foam!

They are like wandering stars that no longer shine as lights in the world. . . .

Remember, my friends, that one day the Lord will come with many thousands of his holy angels to bring judgment. Don't be swayed by these godless people. Don't let them cause divisions among you. The more your faith is ridiculed and persecuted, the tighter you must grip it. Use your grip to gain strength.

Finally, you cannot turn your backs on these misguided souls. You must deal with them: Show mercy. . . . Patiently instruct them in the true faith, so that God may save them. It is possible to love the sinner and hate the sins.

So, what are you supposed to do? . . . (Smile) You do the Christian thing, of course.

What is this story *really* about?

Heresy:

What is heresy? Does it exist in our churches today? What do you think about the idea of the grace of God freeing us to "do as we please?" God, in the Old Testament, dealt harshly with heretics. Read Numbers 14:11-35 and consider how you feel about it.

Unconditional Love:

We're supposed to love sinners and hate their sins. How is that possible? Can we do it without being condescending? Suppose a known prostitute got all dressed up and visited your church one Sunday morning. How would your congregation treat her? How would you treat her?

Let's *talk* about it!

Our Bible begins in the Garden of Eden. It ends in the Holy City. What a magnificent chain of events takes us from one place to the other, from beginning to end!

John the Apostle had a vision. It came to him in a dream and was presented by an angel. The angel got it from Jesus, and Jesus got it from his heavenly Father. It was God's intention to reveal in this manner the wonderful things that would happen to his people. He wanted to give them hope and encouragement, because they were going through terrible times. They were being persecuted and imprisoned for believing in his Son, Jesus. John himself was in prison on the island of Patmos when God sent the revelation. He had plenty of time to write it all down.

At first, John worried that no one would believe him. Many years before, Moses had experienced the same kind of worry. Moses, remember, had doubts about telling the people that God would take them safely out of Egypt.

"Suppose the Israelites do not believe me and will not listen to what I say," Moses said to God. "What shall I do if they say that you did not appear to me?" (Exodus 4:1)

We know that God promised to support Moses with miracles. Would he not in some way support John the Apostle? . . . Ah! No one doubted the inspiration of the prophets. And hadn't Isaiah already prohesied a new Jerusalem? "The new Jerusalem I make will be full of joy, and her people will be happy." (Isaiah 65:18)

John's vision, then, was simply an extension of prophecy, which the people already believed. He would now be able to give them a more detailed view of the future.

So he wrote, just to be sure, "The angel said to me, 'These words are true and can be trusted. And the Lord God, who gives his Spirit to the prophets, has sent his angel to show his servants what must happen very soon.'" (Revelation 22:6)

This is what happened in John's vision:

Like Isaiah, he saw a new heaven and a new earth — not a rebuilding of the old, but something completely new. And, coming down from that new heaven, dressed up as for a wedding, was the most beautiful city anyone could imagine! It was the Holy City, the new Jerusalem.

And a loud voice said, "Now God's home is with mankind! He will live with them, and they shall be his people. . . . He will wipe away all tears from their eyes. There will be no more death, no more grief, or crying or pain. The old things have disappeared."

Then the voice added, "Now I make all things new!"

Next, the angel in John's vision took John to the top of a mountain, so that he would have a clear view. This is what John saw:

The Holy City was shining in perfect triumphant condition! It had a great high wall for security, and John noticed that the wall was made of jasper. This is an opaque quartz that takes on a high shine and was used in making elegant jewelry.

The angel then took out a gold measuring stick and showed John that the Holy City was perfectly proportioned. Around the wall were twelve gates for access, with twelve angels in charge. On the gates were written the names of the twelve tribes of Israel. There were also twelve foundation stones, on which were written the names of the twelve Apostles. These foundation stones were adorned with twelve kinds of precious jewels. Just imagine seeing a foundation wall sparkling with sapphire and emerald and amethyst! And let's not forget pearls — each of the twelve gates was made of a single pearl!

As John in his vision looked into the city, he noticed right away that the street was made of pure gold. What he did not see was a temple, because the Lord God Almighty was the temple. The sun and moon were also missing, but there was no need for either of them, because the city shone with the glory of God.

The angel also showed John the river of the water of life, flowing down the middle of the golden street, coming from the throne of God. On each side of the river was a tree of life, which bears fruit year-round. Its leaves are for the healing of the nations.

It was revealed to John that the greatness and the wealth of the nations would be brought into the city, but nothing impure would enter, including any person who does shameful things or tells lies. Who, then, would be allowed to live in the Holy City? The children of God — those whose names are written in his book of life.

And what of the others — the cowards, traitors, perverts, murderers, the immoral, those who practice magic, those who worship idols? The one who sits on the throne said, "The place for them is the lake burning with fire and sulfur, which is the second death." . . . And John wrote all this down.

The Holy City, revealed to us by God, through Christ, through the angel, and through John the Apostle, is most certainly a paradise. In addition to its riches, it has a river, a tree of life, and fruit, just as the Garden of Eden had. Only the serpent is missing, for the new Jerusalem is free of evil.

Two people enjoyed the first paradise, but — just think! — generations will enjoy the last one! God has said, "I am Alpha and Omega, the beginning and the end." He was there at the beginning, in the Garden of Eden, and he will be there at the end, in the Holy City! Thanks be to God!

(Note: If you are a musician, consider singing or playing the final refrain from "The Holy City"* at this time. Begin softly and slowly; keep the tempo stately throughout, building to a triumphant finish.)

What is this story *really* about?

Orderliness:

God always seems to put things in perfect order. His story goes from paradise to paradise — from the Garden of Eden to the Holy City. Did you ever think about that before? Think about the big difference between the two paradises — the absence of evil in the second one.

Twelve is an important number throughout the Bible, from the twelve tribes of Israel to the twelve apostles. It provides a sense of order. God has given us many examples that suggest we should put order in our lives.

Hope:

It seems like everything went downhill after the serpent did his dirty work in the Garden of Eden. Even though there were times of rallying, they were followed by times of hopelessness. We go through the same thing today — up and down and up again. Jesus was sent, among other things, to bring us hope. What hope do we find in this story of John's vision?

Dreams are wonderful things. Some of them even come true. The best kind are dreams of the future — what we want to do, or be. Can we make dreams come true or does that just happen? If we can make it happen, how do we go about it?

Let's *talk* about it!

"The Holy City" by F. E. Weatherly and Stephen Adams. Published by Carl Fischer Inc. 62 Cooper Square, New York, NY 10003. 1-800-847-4260

Pronunciation Guide

Bible names and places are spelled below in easy-to-read phonetics, according to the following guide:

a	— a, as in ant	igh	— i, as in light
ah	— a, as in ball	ih	— i, as in lip
ai	— a, as in air	oh	— o, as in more
ay	— a, as in say	oo	— o, as in moose
uh	— a, as in around	oo	— u, as in truth
ee	— e, as in evil	ew	— u, as in you
eh	— e, as in method		

Underline indicates accent. Example: <u>uhn</u> - duhr - lighn

Aaron	<u>air</u> - uhn	Antichrist	<u>an</u> - tih - crighst
Achaia	uh - <u>kay</u> - uh	Antioch	<u>an</u> - tih - ahk
Adria	<u>ay</u> - dree - uh	Apphia	<u>ap</u> - fee - ah
Aegean	ih - <u>jee</u> - uhn	Archippus	ahr - <u>kip</u> - uhs
Alpha	<u>al</u> - fuh	Assisi	uh - <u>see</u> - see
Alphaeus	al - <u>fee</u> - uhs	Assyrian	uh - <u>seer</u> - ee - uhn
Amaziah	ah - muh - <u>zigh</u> - uh	Azazel	uh - <u>zay</u> - zel
Amos	<u>ay</u> - muhs		

Baal	bayl	Bartholomew	bahr - <u>thal</u> - uh - mew
Babylon	<u>bab</u> - ih - lahn	Belshazzar	behl - <u>shaz</u> - uhr
Babylonia	bab - ih - <u>lohn</u> - ee - uh	Berytus	beh - <u>right</u> - uhs
Balaam	<u>bay</u> - lahm	Bethel	<u>behth</u> - uhl
Bamoth	<u>bay</u> - muth	Bethlehem	<u>behth</u> - leh - hehm
Barak	<u>bair</u> - uhk	Bildad	<u>bihl</u> - dad

Canaan	<u>kay</u> - nuhn	Colossians	kah - <u>lah</u> - shehnz
Canaanite	<u>kay</u> - nuh - night	Corinth	<u>kohr</u> - ihnth
Carpus	<u>kahr</u> - puhs	Crescens	<u>krehs</u> - ehnz
Colophon	<u>kahl</u> - uh - fahn	Cretans	<u>kree</u> - tehnz
Colossae	kah - <u>lah</u> - see	Crete	kreet

Dalmatia	dal - <u>may</u> - shuh	Delilah	deh - <u>ligh</u> - luh
Damascus	duh - <u>mask</u> - uhs	Demas	<u>dee</u> - muhs

Darius	duh - righ - uhs	Diotrephes	digh - ah - treh - feez
Deborah	dehb - oh - ruh		

Ecclesiastes	eh - klee - zee - ass - teez	Ephesians	eh - fee - zhunz
		Ephesus	ehf - eh - suhs
Eden	ee - dn	Ephriam	ee - free - uhm
Egypt	ee - jihpt	Esau	ee - sah
Elihu	ee - ligh - hew	Ethiopia	eeth - ee - oh - pee - ah
Elijah	ee - ligh - juh	Eunice	yew - nihs
Eliphaz	ehl - ih - faz	Euphrates	yew - fray - teez
Elisha	ee - ligh - shuh	Evilmerodach	eevil - meh - roh - dahk
Epaphras	ehp - uh - fruhs		
Epaphroditus	ee - paf - roh - digh - tuhs	Ezekiel	ee - zeek - yehl

Galatia	gah - lay - shuh	Gentiles	jehn - tiles
Galilee	gal - ih - lee	Gomer	goh - muhr
Gaul	gahl	Gomorrah	goh - mohr - uh

Haggai	hag - ay - igh	Hosea	hoh - zay - uh

Ignatius	ihg - nay - shus	Israelites	ihz - rehl - ights
Isaiah	igh - zay - uh	Issachar	ihs - uh - kahr
Isis	igh - sihs		

Jabbok	jab - ahk	Jezreel	jehz - ree - ehl
Jacob	jay - cuhb	Job	johb
Jael	jay - ehl	Joel	johl
Jairus	jay - ih - ruhs	Jonah	joh - nuh
Jehoash	jeh - hoh - ash	Jordan	johr - dn
Jehoiachin	jeh - hoi - uh - kihn	Joshua	jah - shoo - uh
Jehoiakim	jeh - hoi - uh - kihm	Josiah	joh - sigh - uh
Jeremiah	jair - uh - migh - uh	Judah	joo - duh
Jericho	jair - ih - koh	Judas Iscariot	joo - duhs
Jeroboam	jair - oh - boh - uhm		ihs - kair - ee - aht
Jerusalem	jeh - roo - suh - lehm	Jude	jood
Jezebel	jehz - uh - behl	Justus	juhs - tuhs

Koheleth	koh - <u>hehl</u> - ehth		
Lebanon	<u>lehb</u> - uh - nahn	Lois	<u>loh</u> - ihs
Levite	<u>lee</u> - vight	Lycus	<u>ligh</u> - kuhs
Macedonia	mass - eh - <u>doh</u> - nee - uh	*Mene**	<u>meen</u> - ih
		Messiah	meh - <u>sigh</u> - uh
Machir	<u>may</u> - kihr	Micah	<u>migh</u> - cah
Malachi	<u>mal</u> - uh - kigh	Miriam	<u>mihr</u> - ee - uhm
Matthias	muh - <u>thigh</u> - uhs	Moab	<u>moh</u> - uhb
Mede	meed	Moabite	<u>moh</u> - uh - bight
Melchizedek	mehl - <u>kihz</u> - eh - dehk	Moses	<u>moh</u> - zihs
Memucan	mee - <u>mew</u> - can		
Nahum	<u>nay</u> - huhm	Nebuchadnezzar	nehb - uh - cuhd - <u>nehz</u> - uhr
Naphtali	<u>naf</u> - tih - ligh		
Nazareth	<u>naz</u> - uh - rehth	Nicodemus	nihk - oh - <u>dee</u> - muhs
		Nineveh	<u>nihn</u> - eh - veh
Onesimus	oh - <u>nehs</u> - ih - muhs		
*Parsin**	<u>pahr</u> - sihn	Philemon	fih - <u>lee</u> - muhn
Patmos	<u>pat</u> - muhs	Phillipi	<u>fihl</u> - ih - pigh
Peor	<u>pee</u> - ohr	Phoebe	<u>fee</u> - bee
Persia	<u>puhr</u> - zhuh	Phrygia	<u>frihj</u> - ee - uh
Pharaoh	<u>fair</u> - oh	Pisgah	<u>pihz</u> - guh
Pharisees	<u>fair</u> - ih - seez		
Rahab	<u>ray</u> - hub		
Samaritan	suh - <u>mair</u> - ih - tuhn	Sisera	<u>sihs</u> - eh - ruh
Satan	<u>say</u> - tuhn	Sodom	<u>sah</u> - duhm
Saul	sahl	Solomon	<u>sahl</u> - oh - muhn
Sharon	<u>shair</u> - uhn	Syria	<u>sihr</u> - ih - uh
Sheba	<u>shee</u> - buh		

Tabor	tay - behr	Thrace	thrays
Tarsus	tahr - suhs	Titus	tigh - tuhs
Tekel*	teh - kehl	Troas	troh - az
Thaddaeus	thad - ee - uhs	Tychicus	tihk - ih - kuhs
Thessalonica	thehs - uh - loh - nigh - kuh		
Uzziah	oo - zigh - uh		
Vashti	vash - tigh	Vienne	vee - ehn
Xerxes	zehrk - seez		
Zachary	zak - uh - ree	Zeus	zoos
Zebulun	zehb - yew - luhn	Zophar	zoh - fuhr
Zechariah	zehk - uh - righ - uh		

*Italics denote foreign words, not names.

Appendix

INSTITUTE ON STORYTELLING SKILLS FOR MINISTRY

Storyfest Productions, 3901 Cathedral Ave., NW, #608, Washington, DC 20016. Sponsors travel seminars to such places as England, Wales, and Ireland. Also sponsors stateside seminars.

INTERNATIONAL NETWORK OF BIBLICAL STORYTELLERS

1810 Harvard Blvd., Dayton, OH 45406. A confederation of lay people, clergy, and Bible scholars. Publishes NOBS NEWS and a *Journal of Biblical Storytelling*. Also operates a computer bulletin board to facilitate communication among members. Annual meetings, chapter meetings, festivals.

JEWISH STORYTELLING CENTER

92nd Street Y Library, 1395 Lexington Ave., New York, NY 10128. Will pronounce Hebrew or Aramaic names or words on tape. Send request, a blank cassette, and two dollars for return postage.

NAPPS (NATIONAL ASSOCIATION FOR THE PRESERVATION AND PERPETUATION OF STORYTELLING)

P. O. Box 309, Jonesborough, TN 37659. Sponsors the annual National Storytelling Festival. Publishes "Storytelling Magazine," "Yarnspinner" (a newsletter), and a directory of storytellers. Offers opportunities for learning, through the National Storytelling Institute and the National Congress of Storytelling.

PHOENIX POWER & LIGHT CO., INC.

Drawer C, Odenton, MD 21113. In addition to storytelling, Phoenix focuses on the use of clowning, mime, puppetry, worship, and dance "in settings where people touch people — churches, synagogues, hospitals, nursing homes, schools, libraries, and therapeutic settings." Holds national and regional conferences, has a membership network, publishes an extensive resource manual, a newsletter ("Phoenix Rising"), and maintains a mail-order bookstore.

THE STORYTELLERS SCHOOL OF TORONTO

412-A College St., Toronto, Ontario M5T-1T3, Canada. Sponsors The Toronto Festival of Storytelling. Also publishes books, cassettes, and "Appleseed," a newsletter.

T.A.L.E.S. (THE ALBERTA LEAGUE ENCOURAGING STORYTELLING)

c/o Wordworks, 10523 100 Ave., Edmonton Alberta T5J-0A8, Canada. A province-wide organization for people from all walks of life. Offers a wide variety of workshops and programs. Publishes "Taleteller," a newsletter.

Bibliography

Cassady, Marsh. *Storytelling Step by Step*. San Jose, CA: Resource Publications, Inc., 1990.

Good News Bible. New York: American Bible Society, 1976.

Harrell, John. *A Storyteller's Omnibus*. Kensington, CA: York House, 1985.

Harvey, A. E. *The New English Bible Companion to the New Testament*. England: Oxford University Press and Cambridge University Press, 1970.

Henry, Matthew. *Commentary on the Whole Bible*. Grand Rapids: Zondervan Publishing House, 1961.

Interpreter's Bible, The. New York and Nashville; Abingdon-Cokesbury Press, 1952.

Interpreter's Dictionary of the Bible, The. Four volumes. New York and Nashville: Abingdon Press, 1962.

Oxendine, Jill. "Forum," *Yarnspinner*, Vol. 14, No. 6, p. 8.

Schimmel, Nancy. *Just Enough to Make a Story*. Berkeley, CA: Sisters' Choice Press, 1978.

Schram, Peninnah. *Jewish Stories One Generation Tells Another*. Northvale, NJ: Jason Aronson, Inc., 1987.

Shedlock, Marie L. *The Art of the Story-Teller*. New York: Dover Publications, Inc., 1951.

Smith, Jimmy Neil, ed. *Homespun*. New York: Crown Publishers, Inc., 1988.

Stotter, Ruth. "Enhancing Your Stories With Puppets," *Yarnspinner*, Vol. 14, No. 6, p. 5.

Tenney, Merrill C., general editor. *The Zondervan Pictorial Bible Dictionary*. Grand Rapids: Zondervan Publishing House, 1963.

White, William R. *Speaking in Stories*. Minneapolis: Augsburg Publishing House, 1982.

Whiting, John D. "Jerusalem's Locust Plague," *The National Geographic Magazine*, Vol. XXVIII, No. 6. (December, 1915).

ABOUT THE AUTHOR

Photo by Dyess-Tidwell Studio

Janet Litherland is the author of several works reflecting the arts in ministry, including plays, monologs, mime skits, Readers Theatre scripts, and liturgical dance choreography. Her books include *Absolutely Unforgettable Parties, Getting Started in Drama Ministry, The Complete Banner Handbook, Everything New and Who's Who in Clown Ministry,* and *The Clown Ministry Handbook,* a bestseller.

Janet and her husband, Jerry, live in Georgia. They have two grown sons, Mark and Steve.

ORDER FORM

MERIWETHER PUBLISHING LTD.
P.O. BOX 7710
COLORADO SPRINGS, CO 80933
TELEPHONE: (719) 594-4422

Please send me the following books:

_____**Storytelling From the Bible #CC-B145**   **$10.95**
by Janet Litherland
The art of biblical storytelling

_____**Getting Started in Drama Ministry #CC-B154**   **$9.95**
by Janet Litherland
A complete guide to Christian drama

_____**Everything New and Who's Who in**
Clown Ministry #CC-B126   **$10.95**
by Janet Litherland
Profiles of clown ministers plus 75 skits for special days

_____**The Clown Ministry Handbook #CC-B163**   **$10.95**
by Janet Litherland
The first and most complete text on the art of clown ministry

_____**The Complete Banner Handbook #CC-B172**   **$12.95**
by Janet Litherland
A complete guide to banner design and construction

_____**Absolutely Unforgettable Parties #CC-B135**   **$9.95**
by Janet Litherland
23 great party themes for all seasons

_____**The Official Sunday School Teachers**
Handbook #CC-B152   **$9.95**
by Joanne Owens
An indispensable aid for anyone involved in Sunday school activities

**These and other fine Meriwether Publishing books are available in
your local Christian bookstore or direct from the publisher. Use the
handy order form on this page.**

*I understand that I may return any book
for a full refund if not satisfied.*

NAME: _____

ORGANIZATION NAME: _____

ADDRESS: _____

CITY: _____ STATE: _____ ZIP: _____

PHONE: _____

☐ **Check Enclosed**
☐ **Visa or MasterCard #** _____

Signature: _____ *Expiration*
                                        Date: _____
          (required for Visa/MasterCard orders)

COLORADO RESIDENTS: Please add 3% sales tax.
SHIPPING: Include $1.95 for the first book and 50¢ for each additional book ordered.

☐ *Please send me a copy of your complete catalog of books and plays.*